Edited by Jessie B. Rittenhouse

THE SECOND BOOK OF MODERN VERSE.
THE LITTLE BOOK OF AMERICAN POETS.
THE LITTLE BOOK OF MODERN VERSE.

HOUGHTON MIFFLIN COMPANY
BOSTON AND NEW YORK

THE SECOND BOOK
OF MODERN VERSE

THE SECOND BOOK OF MODERN VERSE

A
SELECTION FROM THE WORK
OF CONTEMPORANEOUS
AMERICAN POETS

EDITED BY
JESSIE B. RITTENHOUSE

BOSTON AND NEW YORK
HOUGHTON MIFFLIN COMPANY
The Riverside Press Cambridge

COPYRIGHT, 1919, BY JESSIE B. RITTENHOUSE

ALL RIGHTS RESERVED

EIGHTH IMPRESSION, MARCH, 1926

The Riverside Press
CAMBRIDGE · MASSACHUSETTS
PRINTED IN THE U.S.A.

FOREWORD

IT was my intention, when preparing *The Little Book of Modern Verse*, published in 1913, to continue the series by a volume once in five years, but as it seemed inadvisable to issue one during the war, it is now six years since the publication of the first volume.

In the meantime, that the series might cover the period of American poetry from the beginning, *The Little Book of American Poets* was edited, confined chiefly to work of the nineteenth century, but ending with a group of living poets whose work has fallen equally within our own period. This group, including Edwin Markham, Bliss Carman, Edith Thomas, Louise Imogen Guiney, Lizette Woodworth Reese, and many others whose work has enriched both periods, was fully represented also in *The Little Book of Modern Verse;* and it has seemed necessary, therefore, keenly as I regret the necessity, which limits of space impose, to omit the work of all poets who have been represented in both of my former collections.

Indeed the period covered by the present volume has been so prolific that it became necessary, if one would represent it with even approximate adequacy, to forego including many poets from *The Little Book of Modern Verse* itself, and but twenty-eight are repeated from that collection.

Even with these necessary eliminations in the interest of space for newer poets, the general scheme of the series — that of small, intimate volumes that shall be typical of the period, rather than exhaustive — has made it impossible to include all whose work I should otherwise have been glad to represent.

While I have not hesitated, where a poet's earlier work seemed finer and more characteristic than his later, to draw upon such earlier work, in the main *The Second Book of Modern Verse* has been selected from poetry published since 1913, the date of my first anthology.

JESSIE B. RITTENHOUSE

NEW YORK
September 23, 1919

CONTENTS

CONTENTS

ACKNOWLEDGMENTS

THANKS are due to the following publishers, editors, and individual owners of copyright for their kind permission to include selections from the volumes enumerated below:

To the estate of Edmund Brooks for a selection from "A Lark Went Singing," by Ruth Guthrie Harding.

To the Century Company for selections from "Trails Sunward," "Wraiths and Realities," and "Collected Poems" of Cale Young Rice; "Challenge" by Louis Untermeyer; "Songs for the New Age" and "War and Laughter" by James Oppenheim; and for "After Sunset" by Grace Hazard Conkling, from the *Century Magazine*.

To the Cornhill Company for selections from "The Divine Image," by Caroline Giltinan.

To Messrs. E. P. Dutton & Co. for selections from "The Retinue, and Other Poems," by Katharine Lee Bates (copyright, 1918), "Lanterns in Gethsemane," by Willard Wattles (copyright, 1918), and "The Earth Turns South," by Clement Wood (copyright, 1919).

To Messrs. Dodd, Mead & Co. for selections from "A Masque of Poets," edited by Edward J. O'Brien.

To Messrs. George H. Doran Company for selections from "Joyce Kilmer: Poems, Essays and Letters," edited by Robert Cortes Holliday (copyright, 1918); "Candles That Burn," by Aline Kilmer (copyright, 1919); "The Dreamers," by Theodosia Garrison (copyright, 1917); "Fifes and Drums" (copyright, 1917); "The Roadside Fire" (copyright, 1912) and "In Deep Places" (copyright, 1914). by Amelia Josephine Burr; "To-Day and To-Morrow" (copyright, 1916) and "World of Windows" (copyright, 1919), by Charles Hanson Towne.

To The Four Seas Company for selections from "The Charnel Rose," by Conrad Aiken.

To Messrs. Henry Holt & Co. for selections from "North

of Boston" and "Mountain Interval," by Robert Frost; "Chicago Poems" and "Cornhuskers," by Carl Sandburg; "These Times," by Louis Untermeyer; "Portraits and Protests," by Sarah N. Cleghorn; "The Factories, and Other Poems" and "The Old Road to Paradise," by Margaret Widdemer; and "My Ireland," by Francis Carlin.

To Messrs. Houghton Mifflin Company for selections from "Rose of the Wind," by Anna Hempstead Branch; "The Singing Leaves" and "Harvest Moon," by Josephine Preston Peabody; "A Sister of the Wind," by Grace Fallow Norton; "Sea Garden," by H. D.; for the poem "Lincoln," by John Gould Fletcher, from "Some Imagist Poets, 1917"; "In the High Hills," by Maxwell Struthers Burt; "Old Christmas and Other Kentucky Tales," by William Aspinwall Bradley; "Turns and Movies," by Conrad Aiken; "A Lonely Flute," by Odell Shepherd; "Idols," by Walter Conrad Arensberg; and to the *Atlantic Monthly* for the use of "The Ancient Beautiful Things" and "The Narrow Doors," by Fannie Stearns Davis.

To Messrs. Harper & Bros. for selections from "Poems," by Dana Burnet, "The Mirthful Lyre," by Arthur Guiterman, and for the poem "There Will Come Soft Rain," by Sara Teasdale, from *Harper's Magazine*.

To Mr. B. W. Huebsch for selections from "Growing Pains," by Jean Starr Untermeyer, and "The Vaunt of Man," by William Ellery Leonard.

To Mr. Mitchell Kennerley for selections from "Renascence and Other Poems," by Edna St. Vincent Millay; "Sonnets of a Portrait Painter" and "The Man on the Hill-Top," by Arthur Davison Ficke; and for the poems, "Blind," by Harry Kemp, and "The Wanderer," by Zoë Akins.

To Mr. Alfred A. Knopf for selections from "Asphalt," by Orrick Johns; "Mushrooms," by Alfred Kreymborg; and "Profiles from China," by Eunice Tietjens.

To the John Lane Company for selections from "Forward, March," by Angela Morgan; "Songs of the Celtic Past," by Norreys Jephson O'Conor; "Singing Fires of Erin," by Eleanor Rogers Cox; and "Gardens Overseas," by Thomas Walsh.

To The Macmillan Company for selections from "The Man Against the Sky," by Edwin Arlington Robinson;

"General William Booth Enters into Heaven, and Other Poems," "The Congo, and Other Poems," and "The Chinese Nightingale and Other Poems," by Vachel Lindsay; "Songs and Satires" and "Spoon River Anthology," by Edgar Lee Masters; "Sword Blades and Poppy Seed," "Men, Women and Ghosts," and "Pictures of the Floating World," by Amy Lowell; "Love Songs," by Sara Teasdale; "Poems and Ballads," by Hermann Hagedorn; "The Story of Eleusis," by Louis V. Ledoux; "The New Day," by Scudder Middleton; "The Drums in Our Street," by Mary Carolyn Davies; and "The Quest," by John G. Neihardt.

To The Midland Press for a selection from "Barbed Wire," by Edwin Ford Piper.

To Mr. Thomas B. Mosher for selections from "The Voice in the Silence," by Thomas S. Jones, Jr.

To Messrs. John P. Morton & Co. for selections from "A Flame in the Wind," by Margaret Steele Anderson.

To The Manas Press for selections from "Verse" by Adelaide Crapsey.

To Messrs. G. P. Putnam's Sons for selections from "The Shadow of Ætna," by Louis V. Ledoux.

To Messrs. Small, Maynard & Co. for selections from "White Fountains," by Edward J. O'Brien.

To Mr. A. M. Robertson for the use of the poem, "Omnium Exeunt," by George Sterling.

To Messrs. Charles Scribner's Sons for selections from "Path-Flower," by Olive Tilford Dargan; "The Children of the Night," by Edwin Arlington Robinson; "One Woman to Another" and "Service and Sacrifice," by Corinne Roosevelt Robinson; "Poems," by Alan Seeger; "Dust and Light," by John Hall Wheelock; and for the poems, "Eye-Witness," by Ridgely Torrence, and "In the Hospital," by Arthur Guiterman, from *Scribner's Magazine*.

To Messrs. Smith & Sale for selections from "Threnodies," by John Myers O'Hara.

To Messrs. Frederick A. Stokes Company for selections from "Grenstone Poems," by Witter Bynner.

To Mr. Robert J. Shores for selections from "The Loves and Losses of Pierrot," by William Griffith.

To Mr. James T. White for selections from "City Pastorals," by William Griffith.

To The Wilmarth Company for selections from "The Shadow Eater," by Benjamin De Casseres.

To the Yale University Press for selections from "The Falconer of God" and "The Burglar of the Zodiac," by William Rose Benét; "Young Adventure" by Stephen Vincent Benét, and "Blue Smoke," by Karl Wilson Baker.

To the *Yale Review* for the use of "Open Windows," by Sara Teasdale.

To Miss Harriet Monroe, editor of *Poetry: A Magazine of Verse,* for the use of the following selections: "Indian Summer," by William Ellery Leonard; "Song," "Let It Be Forgotten," by Sara Teasdale; "The Mould," by Gladys Cromwell; "Ellis Park," by Helen Hoyt; "Harbury," by Louise Driscoll; "Muy Vieja Mexicana," by Alice Corbin Henderson; "Hrolf's Thrall," by Willard Wattles; "Invocation," by Clara Shanafelt; "Peace" and "Convention," by Agnes Lee; "The Millet Plot," by Muna Lee; "Students," by Florence Wilkinson; "Tampico," by Grace Hazard Conkling; "To a Portrait of Whistler in the Brooklyn Art Museum," by Eleanor Rogers Cox; and "April — North Carolina" and "The Water Ouzel," by Harriet Monroe.

To William Stanley Braithwaite for the use of "Spring," by John Gould Fletcher, first published in *The Poetry Review of America.*

To Charles Wharton Stork, editor of *Contemporary Verse,* for "April on the Battlefields," by Leonora Speyer; "Songs of an Empty House," by Marguerite Wilkinson; and for permission to use his own poems, "Death — Divination," and "The Silent Folk."

To *Everybody's Magazine* for permission to use "A Song of Two Wanderers," by Marguerite Wilkinson, and "Old Ships," by David Morton.

To the *Nation* for "A Note from the Pipes," by Leonora Speyer.

To Mahlon Leonard Fisher, editor of *The Sonnet,* for the use of his poems, "Afterwards" and "Old Amaze."

To the *Outlook* for "The White Comrade," by Robert Haven Schauffler.

To the *New Republic* for "The Son," by Ridgely Torrence.

To the *Bellman* for "The Kings are passing Deathward," by David Morton.

THE SECOND BOOK
OF MODERN VERSE

THE ROAD NOT TAKEN

Two roads diverged in a yellow wood,
And sorry I could not travel both
And be one traveler, long I stood
And looked down one as far as I could
To where it bent in the undergrowth;

Then took the other, as just as fair,
And having perhaps the better claim,
Because it was grassy and wanted wear;
Though as for that the passing there
Had worn them really about the same,

And both that morning equally lay
In leaves no step had trodden black.
Oh, I kept the first for another day!
Yet knowing how way leads on to way,
I doubted if I should ever come back.

I shall be telling this with a sigh
Somewhere ages and ages hence:
Two roads diverged in a wood, and I —
I took the one less traveled by,
And that has made all the difference.

Robert Frost

SYMBOL

My faith is all a doubtful thing,
    Wove on a doubtful loom, —
Until there comes, each showery spring,
    A cherry-tree in bloom;

And Christ who died upon a tree
    That death had stricken bare,
Comes beautifully back to me,
    In blossoms, everywhere.

David Morton

SPRING

At the first hour, it was as if one said, "Arise."
At the second hour, it was as if one said, "Go forth."
And the winter constellations that are like patient
    ox-eyes
Sank below the white horizon at the north.

At the third hour, it was as if one said, "I thirst";
At the fourth hour, all the earth was still:
Then the clouds suddenly swung over, stooped, and
    burst;
And the rain flooded valley, plain and hill.

At the fifth hour, darkness took the throne;
At the sixth hour, the earth shook and the wind
    cried;
At the seventh hour, the hidden seed was sown;
At the eighth hour, it gave up the ghost and died.

At the ninth hour, they sealed up the tomb;
And the earth was then silent for the space of three
    hours.
But at the twelfth hour, a single lily from the gloom
Shot forth, and was followed by a whole host of
    flowers.

John Gould Fletcher

" THERE WILL COME SOFT RAIN "

THERE will come soft rain and the smell of the ground,
And swallows circling with their shimmering sound;

And frogs in the pools singing at night,
And wild plum-trees in tremulous white;

Robins will wear their feathery fire
Whistling their whims on a low fence-wire.

And not one will know of the war, not one
Will care at last when it is done.

Not one would mind, neither bird nor tree,
If mankind perished utterly.

And Spring herself when she woke at dawn,
Would scarcely know that we were gone.

Sara Teasdale

SPRING SONG

SOFTLY at dawn a whisper stole
   Down from the Green House on the Hill,
Enchanting many a ghostly bole
   And wood-song with the ancient thrill.

Gossiping on the country-side,
   Spring and the wandering breezes say,
God has thrown Heaven open wide
   And let the thrushes out to-day.

William Griffith

THE DAY BEFORE APRIL

THE day before April
   Alone, alone,
I walked in the woods
   And I sat on a stone.

I sat on a broad stone
   And sang to the birds.
The tune was God's making
   But I made the words.

              Mary Carolyn Davies

BERKSHIRES IN APRIL

IT is not Spring — not yet —
But at East Schaghticoke I saw an ivory birch
Lifting a filmy red mantle of knotted buds
Above the rain-washed whiteness of her arms.

It is not Spring — not yet —
But at Hoosick Falls I saw a robin strutting,
Thin, still, and fidgety,
Not like the puffed, complacent ball of feathers
That dawdles over the cidery Autumn loam.

It is not Spring — not yet —
But up the stocky Pownal hills
Some springy shrub, a scarlet gash on the grayness,
Climbs, flaming, over the melting snows.

It is not Spring — not yet —
But at Williamstown the willows are young and
      golden,

Their tall tips flinging the sun's rays back at him;
And as the sun drags over the Berkshire crests,
The willows glow, the scarlet bushes burn,
The high hill birches shine like purple plumes,
A royal headdress for the brow of Spring.
It is the doubtful, unquiet end of Winter,
And Spring is pulsing out of the wakening soil.

Clement Wood

IN EXCELSIS

SPRING!
And all our valleys turning into green,
Remembering —
As I remember! So my heart turns glad
For so much youth and joy — this to have had
When in my veins the tide of living fire
Was at its flow;
This to know,
When now the miracle of young desire
Burns on the hills, and Spring's sweet choristers
again
Chant from each tree and every bush aflame
Love's wondrous name;
This under youth's glad reign,
With all the valleys turning into green —
This to have heard and seen!

And Song!
Once to have known what every wakened bird
Has heard;
Once to have entered into that great harmony
Of love's creation, and to feel
The pulsing waves of wonder steal

Through all my being; once to be
In that same sea
Of wakened joy that stirs in every tree
And every bird; and then to sing —
To sing aloud the endless Song of Spring!

Waiting, I turn to Thee,
Expectant, humble, and on bended knee;
Youth's radiant fire
Only to burn at Thy unknown desire —
For this alone has Song been granted me.
Upon Thy altar burn me at Thy will;
All wonders fill
My cup, and it is Thine;
Life's precious wine
For this alone: for Thee.
Yet never can be paid
The debt long laid
Upon my heart, because my lips did press
In youth's glad Spring the Cup of Loveliness!

Thomas S. Jones, Jr.

BLUE SQUILLS

How many million Aprils came
    Before I ever knew
How white a cherry bough could be,
    A bed of squills, how blue.

And many a dancing April
    When life is done with me,
Will lift the blue flame of the flower
    And the white flame of the tree.

Oh, burn me with your beauty, then,
 Oh, hurt me, tree and flower,
Lest in the end death try to take
 Even this glistening hour.

O shaken flowers, O shimmering trees,
 O sunlit white and blue,
Wound me, that I through endless sleep
 May bear the scar of you.

Sara Teasdale

EARTH

GRASSHOPPER, your fairy song
And my poem alike belong
To the dark and silent earth
From which all poetry has birth;
All we say and all we sing
Is but as the murmuring
Of that drowsy heart of hers
When from her deep dream she stirs:
If we sorrow, or rejoice,
You and I are but her voice.

Deftly does the dust express
In mind her hidden loveliness,
And from her cool silence stream
The cricket's cry and Dante's dream;
For the earth that breeds the trees
Breeds cities too, and symphonies.
Equally her beauty flows
Into a savior, or a rose —

Looks down in dream, and from above
Smiles at herself in Jesus' love.
Christ's love and Homer's art
Are but the workings of her heart;
Through Leonardo's hand she seeks
Herself, and through Beethoven speaks
In holy thunderings around
The awful message of the ground.

The serene and humble mold
Does in herself all selves enfold —
Kingdoms, destinies, and creeds,
Great dreams, and dauntless deeds,
Science that metes the firmament,
The high, inflexible intent
Of one for many sacrificed —
Plato's brain, the heart of Christ:
All love, all legend, and all lore
Are in the dust forevermore.

Even as the growing grass
Up from the soil religions pass,
And the field that bears the rye
Bears parables and prophecy.
Out of the earth the poem grows
Like the lily, or the rose;
And all man is, or yet may be,
Is but herself in agony
Toiling up the steep ascent
Toward the complete accomplishment
When all dust shall be, the whole
Universe, one conscious soul.
Yea, the quiet and cool sod
Bears in her breast the dream of God.

If you would know what earth is, scan
The intricate, proud heart of man,
Which is the earth articulate,
And learn how holy and how great,
How limitless and how profound
Is the nature of the ground —
How without terror or demur
We may entrust ourselves to her
When we are wearied out, and lay
Our faces in the common clay.

For she is pity, she is love,
All wisdom she, all thoughts that move
About her everlasting breast
Till she gathers them to rest:
All tenderness of all the ages,
Seraphic secrets of the sages,
Vision and hope of all the seers,
All prayer, all anguish, and all tears
Are but the dust, that from her dream
Awakes, and knows herself supreme —
Are but earth when she reveals
All that her secret heart conceals
Down in the dark and silent loam,
Which is ourselves, asleep, at home.

Yea, and this, my poem, too,
Is part of her as dust and dew,
Wherein herself she doth declare
Through my lips, and say her prayer.

John Hall Wheelock

TREES

I THINK that I shall never see
A poem lovely as a tree.

A tree whose hungry mouth is prest
Against the earth's sweet flowing breast;

A tree that looks at God all day,
And lifts her leafy arms to pray;

A tree that may in summer wear
A nest of robins in her hair;

Upon whose bosom snow has lain;
Who intimately lives with rain.

Poems are made by fools like me,
But only God can make a tree.

Joyce Kilmer

IDEALISTS

BROTHER Tree:
Why do you reach and reach?
Do you dream some day to touch the sky?
Brother Stream:
Why do you run and run?
Do you dream some day to fill the sea?
Brother Bird:
Why do you sing and sing?
Do you dream —
Young Man:
Why do you talk and talk and talk?

Alfred Kreymborg

BLIND

THE Spring blew trumpets of color;
Her Green sang in my brain —
I heard a blind man groping
"Tap — tap" with his cane;

I pitied him in his blindness;
But can I boast, "I see" ?
Perhaps there walks a spirit
Close by, who pities me, —

A spirit who hears me tapping
The five-sensed cane of mind
Amid such unguessed glories —
That I am worse than blind.

Harry Kemp

YELLOW WARBLERS

THE first faint dawn was flushing up the skies
When, dreamland still bewildering mine eyes,
I looked out to the oak that, winter-long,
— a winter wild with war and woe and wrong —
Beyond my casement had been void of song.

And lo! with golden buds the twigs were set,
Live buds that warbled like a rivulet
Beneath a veil of willows. Then I knew
Those tiny voices, clear as drops of dew,
Those flying daffodils that fleck the blue,

Those sparkling visitants from myrtle isles,
Wee pilgrims of the sun, that measure miles

Innumerable over land and sea
With wings of shining inches. Flakes of glee,
They filled that dark old oak with jubilee,

Foretelling in delicious roundelays
Their dainty courtships on the dipping sprays,
How they should fashion nests, mate helping mate,
Of milkweed flax and fern-down delicate
To keep sky-tinted eggs inviolate.

Listening to those blithe notes, I slipped once more
From lyric dawn through dreamland's open door,
And there was God, Eternal Life that sings,
Eternal joy, brooding all mortal things,
A nest of stars, beneath untroubled wings.

Katharine Lee Bates

APRIL — NORTH CAROLINA

Would you not be in Tryon
    Now that the spring is here,
When mocking-birds are praising
    The fresh, the blossomy year?

Look — on the leafy carpet
    Woven of winter's browns
Iris and pink azaleas
    Flutter their gaudy gowns.

The dogwood spreads white meshes —
    So white and light and high —
To catch the drifting sunlight
    Out of the cobalt sky.

The pointed beech and maple,
  The pines, dark-tufted, tall,
Pattern with many colors
  The mountain's purple wall.

Hark — what a rushing torrent
  Of crystal song falls sheer!
Would you not be in Tryon
  Now that the spring is here?

                         Harriet Monroe

PATH FLOWER

A RED-CAP sang in Bishop's wood,
  A lark o'er Golder's lane,
As I the April pathway trod
  Bound west for Willesden.

At foot each tiny blade grew big
  And taller stood to hear,
And every leaf on every twig
  Was like a little ear.

As I too paused, and both ways tried
  To catch the rippling rain, —
So still, a hare kept at my side
  His tussock of disdain, —

Behind me close I heard a step,
  A soft pit-pat surprise,
And looking round my eyes fell deep
  Into sweet other eyes;

The eyes like wells, where sun lies too,
  So clear and trustful brown,
Without a bubble warning you
  That here's a place to drown.

"How many miles?" Her broken shoes
  Had told of more than one.
She answered like a dreaming Muse,
  "I came from Islington."

"So long a tramp?" Two gentle nods,
  Then seemed to lift a wing,
And words fell soft as willow-buds,
  "I came to find the Spring."

A timid voice, yet not afraid
  In ways so sweet to roam,
As it with honey bees had played
  And could no more go home.

Her home! I saw the human lair,
  I heard the huckster's bawl,
I stifled with the thickened air
  Of bickering mart and stall.

Without a tuppence for a ride,
  Her feet had set her free.
Her rags, that decency defied,
  Seemed new with liberty.

But she was frail. Who would might note
  The trail of hungering
That for an hour she had forgot
  In wonder of the Spring.

So shriven by her joy she glowed
  It seemed a sin to chat.
(A tea-shop snuggled off the road;
  Why did I think of that?)

Oh, frail, so frail! I could have wept, —
  But she was passing on,
And I but muddled, "You'll accept
  A penny for a bun?"

Then up her little throat a spray
  Of rose climbed for it must;
A wilding lost till safe it lay
  Hid by her curls of rust;

And I saw modesties at fence
  With pride that bore no name;
So old it was she knew not whence
  It sudden woke and came;

But that which shone of all most clear
  Was startled, sadder thought
That I should give her back the fear
  Of life she had forgot.

And I blushed for the world we'd made,
  Putting God's hand aside,
Till for the want of sun and shade
  His little children died;

And blushed that I who every year
  With Spring went up and down,
Must greet a soul that ached for her
  With "penny for a bun!"

Struck as a thief in holy place
    Whose sin upon him cries,
I watched the flowers leave her face,
    The song go from her eyes.

Then she, sweet heart, she saw my rout,
    And of her charity
A hand of grace put softly out
    And took the coin from me.

A red-cap sang in Bishop's wood,
    A lark o'er Golder's lane;
But I, alone, still glooming stood,
    And April plucked in vain;

Till living words rang in my ears
    And sudden music played:
Out of such sacred thirst as hers
    The world shall be remade.

Afar she turned her head and smiled
    As might have smiled the Spring,
And humble as a wondering child
    I watched her vanishing.
                        Olive Tilford Dargan

LITTLE THINGS

THERE's nothing very beautiful and nothing very gay
About the rush of faces in the town by day,
But a light tan cow in a pale green mead,
That is very beautiful, beautiful indeed . .

And the soft March wind and the low March mist
Are better than kisses in a dark street kissed . . .
The fragrance of the forest when it wakes at dawn,
The fragrance of a trim green village lawn,
The hearing of the murmur of the rain at play —
These things are beautiful, beautiful as day!
And I shan't stand waiting for love or scorn
When the feast is laid for a day new-born . . .
Oh, better let the little things I loved when little
Return when the heart finds the great things brittle;
And better is a temple made of bark and thong
Than a tall stone temple that may stand too long.

Orrick Johns

NEW DREAMS FOR OLD

Is there no voice in the world to come crying,
   "New dreams for old!
   New for old!"?
Many have long in my heart been lying,
   Faded, weary, and cold.
All of them, all, would I give for a new one.
   (Is there no seeker
   Of dreams that were?)
Nor would I ask if the new were a true one:
   Only for new dreams!
   New for old!

For I am here, half way of my journey,
   Here with the old!
   All so old!
And the best heart with death is at tourney,
   If naught new it is told.

Will there no voice, then, come — or a vision —
    Come with the beauty
    That ever blows
Out of the lands that are called Elysian?
    I must have new dreams!
    New for old!

Cale Young Rice

INVOCATION

O Glass-Blower of time,
    Hast blown all shapes at thy fire?
Canst thou no lovelier bell,
    No clearer bubble, clear as delight, inflate me —
Worthy to hold such wine
    As was never yet trod from the grape,
Since the stars shed their light, since the moon
    Troubled the night with her beauty?

Clara Shanafelt

DREAM

But now the Dream has come again, the world is as
    of old.

Once more I feel about my breast the heartening
    splendors fold.

Now I am back in that good place from which my foot-
    steps came,

And I am hushed of any grief and have laid by my
    shame.

I know not by what road I came — oh wonderful and
    fair!

Only I know I ailed for thee and that thou wert not
   there.
Then suddenly Time's stalwart wall before thee did
   divide,
Its solid bastions dreamed and swayed and there was
   I inside.

It is thy nearness makes thee seem so wonderful and
   far.
In that deep sky thou art obscured as in the noon, a
   star.
But when the darkness of my grief swings up the
   mid-day sky,
My need begets a shining world. Lo, in thy light am I.

All that I used to be is there and all I yet shall be.
My laughter deepens in the air, my quiet in the tree.
My utter tremblings of delight are manna from the sky,
And shining flower-like in the grass my innocencies lie.

And here I run and sleep and laugh and have no name
   at all.
Only if God should speak to me then I would heed
   the call.
And I forget the curious ways, the alien looks of men,
For even as it was of old, so is it now again.

Still every angel looks the same and all the folks are
   there
That are so bounteous and mild and have not any care.
But kindest to me is the one I would most choose
   to be.
She is so beautiful and sheds such loving looks on me.

She is so beautiful — and lays her cheek against my
    own.
Back — in the world — they all will say, "How happy
    you have grown."
Her breath is sweet about my eyes and she has healed
    me now,
Though I be scarred with grief, I keep her kiss upon
    my brow.

All day, sweet land, I fight for thee outside the goodly
    wall,
And 'twixt my breathless wounds I have no sight of
    thee at all!
And sometimes I forget thy looks and what thy ways
    may be!
I have denied thou wert at all — yet still I fight for
    thee.

Anna Hempstead Branch

FOUR SONNETS

I

SANCTUARY

How may one hold these days of wonderment
    And bind them into stillness with a thong,
    Ere as a fleeting dream they pass along
Into the waste of lovely things forspent;
How may one keep what the Great Powers have sent,
    The prayers fulfilled more beautiful and strong
    Than any thought could fashion into song
Of all the rarest harmonies inblent?

There is an Altar where they may be laid
   And sealed in Faith within Its sacred care, —
     Here they are safe unto the very end;
For these are of the things that never fade,
   Brought from the City that is built four-square,
     The gifts of Him who is the Perfect Friend.

II

THE LAST SPRING

THE first glad token of the Spring is here
   That bears each time one miracle the more,
   For in the sunlight is the golden ore,
The joyous promise of a waking year;
And in that promise all clouds disappear
   And youth itself comes back as once before,
   For only dreams are real in April's store
When buds are bursting and the skies are clear.

Fair Season! at your touch the sleeping land
   Quickens to rapture, and a rosy flame
     Is the old signal of awakening;
Thus in a mystery I understand
   The deepest meaning of your lovely name —
     How it will be in that perpetual Spring!

III

THE GARDEN

BEHIND the pinions of the Seraphim,
   Whose wings flame out upon the swinging spheres,
   There is a Voice that speaks the numbered years
Until that Day when all comes back to Him;

Behind the faces of the Cherubim,
    Whose smiles of love are seen through broken tears,
    There is a Face that every creature fears,
The Face of Love no veil may ever dim.

O Angels of Glad Laughter and of Song,
    Your voices sound so near, the little wall
        Can scarcely hide the trees that bend and nod;
Unbar the gate, for you have waited long
    To show the Garden that was made for all, —
        Where all is safe beneath the Smile of God.

IV

THE PATH OF THE STARS

Down through the spheres that chant the Name of
        One
    Who is the Law of Beauty and of Light
    He came, and as He came the waiting Night
Shook with the gladness of a Day begun;
And as He came, He said: Thy Will Be Done
    On Earth; and all His vibrant Words were white
    And glistering with silver, and their might
Was of the glory of a rising sun.

Unto the Stars sang out His Living Words
    White and with silver, and their rhythmic sound
        Was as a mighty symphony unfurled;
And back from out the Stars like homing birds
    They fell in love upon the sleeping ground
        And were forever in a wakened world.

Thomas S. Jones, Jr.

CHANSON OF THE BELLS OF OSENÈY
Thirteenth Century

THE bells of Osenèy
(Hautclère, Doucement, Austyn)
Chant sweetly every day,
And sadly, for our sin.
The bells of Osenèy
(John, Gabriel, Marie)
Chant lowly,
       Chant slowly,
Chant wistfully and holy
Of Christ, our Paladin.

Hautclère chants to the East
(His tongue is silvery high),
And Austyn like a priest
Sends west a weighty cry.
But Doucement set between
(Like an appeasive nun)
Chants cheerly,
       Chants clearly,
As if Christ heard her nearly,
A plea to every sky.

A plea that John takes up
(He is the evangelist)
Till Gabriel's angel cup
Pours sound to sun or mist.
And last of all Marie
(The virgin-voice of God)
Peals purely,
       Demurely,
And with a tone so surely
Divine, that all must hear.

The bells of Osenèy
(Doucement, Austyn, Hautclère)
Pour ever day by day
Their peals on the rapt air;
And with their mellow mates
(John, Gabriel, Marie)
Tell slowly,

      Tell lowly,
Of Christ the High and Holy,
Who makes the whole world fair.

          Cale Young Rice

POETS

VAIN is the chiming of forgotten bells
    That the wind sways above a ruined shrine.
Vainer his voice in whom no longer dwells
    Hunger that craves immortal Bread and Wine.

Light songs we breathe that perish with our breath
    Out of our lips that have not kissed the rod.
They shall not live who have not tasted death.
    They only sing who are struck dumb by God.

          Joyce Kilmer

ACCEPTANCE

I CANNOT think nor reason,
I only know he came
With hands and feet of healing
And wild heart all aflame.

With eyes that dimmed and softened
At all the things he saw,

And in his pillared singing
I read the marching Law.

I only know he loves me,
Enfolds and understands —
And oh, his heart that holds me,
And oh, his certain hands!

Willard Wattles

IN THE HOSPITAL

BECAUSE on the branch that is tapping my pane
  A sun-wakened leaf-bud, uncurled,
Is bursting its rusty brown sheathing in twain,
  I know there is Spring in the world.

Because through the sky-patch whose azure and white
  My window frames all the day long,
A yellow-bird dips for an instant of flight,
  I know there is Song.

Because even here in this Mansion of Woe
  Where creep the dull hours, leaden-shod,
Compassion and Tenderness aid me, I know
  There is God.

Arthur Guiterman

OVERNIGHT, A ROSE

THAT overnight a rose could come
  I one time did believe,
For when the fairies live with one,
  They wilfully deceive.
But now I know this perfect thing
  Under the frozen sod

In cold and storm grew patiently
   Obedient to God.
My wonder grows, since knowledge came
   Old fancies to dismiss;
And courage comes. Was not the rose
   A winter doing this?
Nor did it know, the weary while,
   What color and perfume
With this completed loveliness
   Lay in that earthly tomb.
So maybe I, who cannot see
   What God wills not to show,
May, some day, bear a rose for Him
   It took my life to grow.

Caroline Giltinan

THE IDOL-MAKER PRAYS

GREAT god whom I shall carve from this gray stone
   Wherein thou liest, hid to all but me,
Grant thou that when my art hath made thee known
   And others bow, I shall not worship thee.
But, as I pray thee now, then let me pray
   Some greater god, — like thee to be conceived
Within my soul, — for strength to turn away
   From his new altar, when, that task achieved,
He, too, stands manifest. Yea, let me yearn
   From dream to grander dream! Let me not rest
Content at any goal! Still bid me spurn
   Each transient triumph on the Eternal Quest,
Abjuring godlings whom my hand hath made
For Deity, revealed, but unportrayed!

Arthur Guiterman

REVEILLÉ

WHAT sudden bugle calls us in the night
    And wakes us from a dream that we had shaped;
Flinging us sharply up against a fight
    We thought we had escaped.

It is no easy waking, and we win
    No final peace; our victories are few.
But still imperative forces pull us in
    And sweep us somehow through.

Summoned by a supreme and confident power
    That wakes our sleeping courage like a blow,
We rise, half-shaken, to the challenging hour,
    And answer it — and go.

Louis Untermeyer

THE BREAKING

(The Lord God speaks to a youth)

BEND now thy body to the common weight!
(But oh, that vine-clad head, those limbs of morn!
Those proud young shoulders I myself made straight!
How shall ye wear the yoke that must be worn?)

Look thou, my son, what wisdom comes to thee!
(But oh, that singing mouth, those radiant eyes!
Those dancing feet — that I myself made free!
How shall I sadden them to make them wise?)

Nay then, thou shalt! Resist not, have a care!
(Yea, I must work my plans who sovereign sit!
Yet do not tremble so! I cannot bear —
Though I am God — to see thee so submit!)
Margaret Steele Anderson

THE FALCONER OF GOD

I FLUNG my soul to the air like a falcon flying.
I said, "Wait on, wait on, while I ride below!
  I shall start a heron soon
  In the marsh beneath the moon —
A strange white heron rising with silver on its wings,
   Rising and crying
  Wordless, wondrous things;
The secret of the stars, of the world's heart-strings,
  The answer to their woe.
Then stoop thou upon him, and grip and hold him
  so!"

My wild soul waited on as falcons hover.
I beat the reedy fens as I trampled past.
  I heard the mournful loon
  In the marsh beneath the moon.
And then — with feathery thunder — the bird of my
  desire
   Broke from the cover
  Flashing silver fire.
High up among the stars I saw his pinions spire.
  The pale clouds gazed aghast
As my falcon stoopt upon him, and gript and held
  him fast.

My soul dropt through the air — with heavenly plun-
　　der? —
Gripping the dazzling bird my dreaming knew?
　　　Nay! but a piteous freight,
　　　A dark and heavy weight
Despoiled of silver plumage, its voice forever stilled, —
　　　All of the wonder
　　Gone that ever filled
Its guise with glory. Oh, bird that I have killed,
　　How brilliantly you flew
Across my rapturous vision when first I dreamed of
　　you!

　　Yet I fling my soul on high with new endeavor,
　　And I ride the world below with a joyful mind.
　　　I shall start a heron soon
　　　In the marsh beneath the moon —
A wondrous silver heron its inner darkness fledges!
　　　I beat forever
　　The fens and the sedges.
　　The pledge is still the same — for all disastrous
　　pledges,
　　　All hopes resigned!
My soul still flies above me for the quarry it shall find.
　　　　　　　Wm. Rose Benét

DILEMMA

　　WHAT though the moon should come
　　　With a blinding glow,
　　And the stars have a game
　　　On the wood's edge,

A man would have to still
  Cut and weed and sow,
And lay a white line
  When he plants a hedge.

What though God
  With a great sound of rain
Came to talk of violets
  And things people do,
I would have to labor
  And dig with my brain
Still to get a truth
  Out of all words new.

Orrick Johns

TO A PORTRAIT OF WHISTLER IN THE BROOKLYN ART MUSEUM

WHAT waspish whim of Fate
  Was this that bade you here
Hold dim, unhonored state,
  No single courtier near?

Is there, of all who pass,
  No choice, discerning few
To poise the ribboned glass
  And gaze enwrapt on you?

Sword-soul that from its sheath
  Laughed leaping to the fray,
How calmly underneath
  Goes Brooklyn on her way!

Quite heedless of that smile —
  Half-devil and half-god,
Your quite unequalled style,
  The airy heights you trod.

Ah, could you from earth's breast
  Come back to take the air,
What matter here for jest
  Most exquisite and rare!

But since you may not come,
  Since silence holds you fast,
Since all your quips are dumb
  And all your laughter past —

I give you mine instead,
  And something with it too
That Brooklyn leaves unsaid —
  The world's fine homage due.

Ah, Prince, you smile again —
  "My faith, the court is small!"
I know, dear James — but then
  It's I or none at all!

                    Eleanor Rogers Cox

FLAMMONDE [1]

THE man Flammonde, from God knows where,
With firm address and foreign air,
With news of nations in his talk
And something royal in his walk,
With glint of iron in his eyes,
But never doubt, nor yet surprise,

[1] Reprinted, by permission of the publishers, from *The Man against the Sky*, by Edwin Arlington Robinson. Copyright, 1916, by The Macmillan Company.

Appeared, and stayed, and held his head
As one by kings accredited.

Erect, with his alert repose
About him, and about his clothes,
He pictured all tradition hears
Of what we owe to fifty years.
His cleansing heritage of taste
Paraded neither want nor waste;
And what he needed for his fee
To live, he borrowed graciously.

He never told us what he was,
Or what mischance, or other cause,
Had banished him from better days
To play the Prince of Castaways.
Meanwhile he played surpassing well
A part, for most, unplayable;
In fine, one pauses, half afraid
To say for certain that he played.

For that, one may as well forego
Conviction as to yes or no;
Nor can I say just how intense
Would then have been the difference
To several, who, having striven
In vain to get what he was given,
Would see the stranger taken on
By friends not easy to be won.

Moreover, many a malcontent
He soothed and found munificent;
His courtesy beguiled and foiled
Suspicion that his years were soiled;

His mien distinguished any crowd,
His credit strengthened when he bowed;
And women, young and old, were fond
Of looking at the man Flammonde.

There was a woman in our town
On whom the fashion was to frown;
But while our talk renewed the tinge
Of a long-faded scarlet fringe,
The man Flammonde saw none of that,
And what he saw we wondered at —
That none of us, in her distress,
Could hide or find our littleness.

There was a boy that all agreed
Had shut within him the rare seed
Of learning. We could understand,
But none of us could lift a hand.
The man Flammonde appraised the youth,
And told a few of us the truth;
And thereby, for a little gold,
A flowered future was unrolled.

There were two citizens who fought
For years and years, and over nought;
They made life awkward for their friends,
And shortened their own dividends.
The man Flammonde said what was wrong
Should be made right, nor was it long
Before they were again in line,
And had each other in to dine.

And these I mention are but four
Of many out of many more.

So much for them. But what of him —
So firm in every look and limb?
What small satanic sort of kink
Was in his brain? What broken link
Withheld him from the destinies
That came so near to being his?

What was he, when we came to sift
His meaning, and to note the drift
Of incommunicable ways
That make us ponder while we praise?
Why was it that his charm revealed
Somehow the surface of a shield?
What was it that we never caught?
What was he, and what was he not?

How much it was of him we met
We cannot ever know; nor yet
Shall all he gave us quite atone
For what was his, and his alone;
Nor need we now, since he knew best,
Nourish an ethical unrest:
Rarely at once will nature give
The power to be Flammonde and live.

We cannot know how much we learn
From those who never will return,
Until a flash of unforeseen
Remembrance falls on what has been.
We've each a darkening hill to climb;
And this is why, from time to time
In Tilbury Town, we look beyond
Horizons for the man Flammonde.

Edwin Arlington Robinson

THE CHINESE NIGHTINGALE [1]

"How, how," he said. "Friend Chang," I said,
"San Francisco sleeps as the dead —
Ended license, lust and play:
Why do you iron the night away?
Your big clock speaks with a deadly sound,
With a tick and a wail till dawn comes round.
While the monster shadows glower and creep,
What can be better for man than sleep?"

"I will tell you a secret," Chang replied;
"My breast with vision is satisfied,
And I see green trees and fluttering wings,
And my deathless bird from Shanghai sings."
Then he lit five fire-crackers in a pan.
"Pop, pop," said the fire-crackers, "cra-cra-crack."
He lit a joss stick long and black.
Then the proud gray joss in the corner stirred;
On his wrist appeared a gray small bird,
And this was the song of the gray small bird:
"Where is the princess, loved forever,
Who made Chang first of the kings of men?"

And the joss in the corner stirred again;
And the carved dog, curled in his arms, awoke,
Barked forth a smoke-cloud that whirled and broke.
It piled in a maze round the ironing-place,
And there on the snowy table wide
Stood a Chinese lady of high degree,
With a scornful, witching, tea-rose face . . .

[1] Reprinted, by permission of the publishers, from *The Chinese Nightingale, and Other Poems*, by Vachel Lindsay. Copyright, 1917, by The Macmillan Company.

Yet she put away all form and pride,
And laid her glimmering veil aside
With a childlike smile for Chang and for me.

The walls fell back, night was aflower,
The table gleamed in a moonlit bower,
While Chang, with a countenance carved of stone,
Ironed and ironed, all alone.
And thus she sang to the busy man Chang:
"Have you forgotten . . .
Deep in the ages, long, long ago,
I was your sweetheart, there on the sand —
Storm-worn beach of the Chinese land?
We sold our grain in the peacock town
Built on the edge of the sea-sands brown —
Built on the edge of the sea-sands brown . . .

When all the world was drinking blood
From the skulls of men and bulls
And all the world had swords and clubs of stone,
We drank our tea in China beneath the sacred spice
        trees,
And heard the curled waves of the harbor moan.
And this gray bird, in Love's first spring,
With a bright-bronze breast and a bronze-brown wing,
Captured the world with his carolling.
Do you remember, ages after,
At last the world we were born to own?
You were the heir of the yellow throne —
The world was the field of the Chinese man
And we were the pride of the Sons of Han?
We copied deep books and we carved in jade,
And wove blue silks in the mulberry shade . . ."

"I remember, I remember
That Spring came on forever,
That Spring came on forever,"
Said the Chinese nightingale.

My heart was filled with marvel and dream,
Though I saw the western street-lamps gleam,
Though dawn was bringing the western day,
Though Chang was a laundryman ironing away ...
Mingled there with the streets and alleys,
The railroad-yard and the clock-tower bright,
Demon clouds crossed ancient valleys;
Across wide lotus-ponds of light
I marked a giant firefly's flight.

And the lady, rosy-red,
Flourished her fan, her shimmering fan,
Stretched her hand toward Chang, and said:
"Do you remember,
Ages after,
Our palace of heart-red stone?
Do you remember
The little doll-faced children
With their lanterns full of moon-fire,
That came from all the empire
Honoring the throne? —
The loveliest fête and carnival
Our world had ever known?
The sages sat about us
With their heads bowed in their beards,
With proper meditation on the sight.
Confucius was not born;
We lived in those great days

Confucius later said were lived aright . . .
And this gray bird, on that day of spring,
With a bright-bronze breast, and a bronze-brown
      wing,
Captured the world with his carolling.
Late at night his tune was spent.
Peasants,
Sages,
Children,
Homeward went,
And then the bronze bird sang for you and me.
We walked alone. Our hearts were high and free.
I had a silvery name, I had a silvery name,
I had a silvery name — do you remember
The name you cried beside the tumbling sea?"

Chang turned not to the lady slim —
He bent to his work, ironing away;
But she was arch, and knowing and glowing,
And the bird on his shoulder spoke for him.

"Darling . . . darling . . . darling . . . darling . . . "
Said the Chinese nightingale.

The great gray joss on a rustic shelf,
Rakish and shrewd, with his collar awry,
Sang impolitely, as though by himself,
Drowning with his bellowing the nightingale's cry:
"Back through a hundred, hundred years
Hear the waves as they climb the piers,
Hear the howl of the silver seas,
Hear the thunder.
Hear the gongs of holy China

How the waves and tunes combine
In a rhythmic clashing wonder,
Incantation old and fine:
  'Dragons, dragons, Chinese dragons,
    Red fire-crackers, and green fire-crackers,
    And dragons, dragons, Chinese dragons.' "

Then the lady, rosy-red,
Turned to her lover Chang and said:
"Dare you forget that turquoise dawn,
When we stood in our mist-hung velvet lawn,
And worked a spell this great joss taught
Till a God of the Dragons was charmed and caught?
From the flag high over our palace home
He flew to our feet in rainbow-foam —
A king of beauty and tempest and thunder
Panting to tear our sorrows asunder:
A dragon of fair adventure and wonder.
We mounted the back of that royal slave
With thoughts of desire that were noble and grave.
We swam down the shore to the dragon-mountains,
We whirled to the peaks and the fiery fountains.
To our secret ivory house we were borne.
We looked down the wonderful wing-filled regions
Where the dragons darted in glimmering legions.
Right by my breast the nightingale sang;
The old rhymes rang in the sunlit mist
That we this hour regain —
Song-fire for the brain.
When my hands and my hair and my feet you kissed,
When you cried for your heart's new pain,
What was my name in the dragon-mist,
In the rings of rainbowed rain?"

"Sorrow and love, glory and love,"
Said the Chinese nightingale.
"Sorrow and love, glory and love,"
Said the Chinese nightingale.

And now the joss broke in with his song:
"Dying ember, bird of Chang,
Soul of Chang, do you remember? —
Ere you returned to the shining harbor
There were pirates by ten thousand
Descended on the town
In vessels mountain-high and red and brown,
Moon-ships that climbed the storms and cut the
        skies.
On their prows were painted terrible bright eyes.
But I was then a wizard and a scholar and a
        priest;
I stood upon the sand;
With lifted hand I looked upon them
And sunk their vessels with my wizard eyes,
And the stately lacquer-gate made safe again.
Deep, deep below the bay, the sea-weed and the
        spray,
Embalmed in amber every pirate lies,
Embalmed in amber every pirate lies."

Then this did the noble lady say:
"Bird, do you dream of our home-coming day
When you flew like a courier on before
From the dragon-peak to our palace-door,
And we drove the steed in your singing path —
The ramping dragon of laughter and wrath:
And found our city all aglow,

And knighted this joss that decked it so?
There were golden fishes in the purple river
And silver fishes and rainbow fishes.
There were golden junks in the laughing river.
And silver junks and rainbow junks:
There were golden lilies by the bay and river,
And silver lilies and tiger-lilies,
And tinkling wind-bells in the gardens of the
      town
By the black-lacquer gate
Where walked in state
The kind king Chang
And his sweetheart mate . . .
With his flag-born dragon
And his crown of pearl . . . and . . . jade,
And his nightingale reigning in the mulberry
      shade,
And sailors and soldiers on the sea-sands brown,
And priests who bowed them down to your song ⌒
By the city called Han, the peacock town,
By the city called Han, the nightingale town,
The nightingale town."

Then sang the bird, so strangely gay,
Fluttering, fluttering, ghostly and gray,
A vague, unravelling, final tune,
Like a long unwinding silk cocoon;
Sang as though for the soul of him
Who ironed away in that bower dim: —
    "I have forgotten
    Your dragons great,
    Merry and mad and friendly and bold.
    Dim is your proud lost palace-gate.

I vaguely know
There were heroes of old,
Troubles more than the heart could hold,
There were wolves in the woods
Yet lambs in the fold,
Nests in the top of the almond tree . . .
The evergreen tree . . . and the mulberry
        tree . . .
Life and hurry and joy forgotten,
Years on years I but half-remember . . .
Man is a torch, then ashes soon,
May and June, then dead December,
Dead December, then again June.
Who shall end my dream's confusion?
Life is a loom, weaving illusion . . .
I remember, I remember
There were ghostly veils and laces . . .
In the shadowy bowery places . . .
With lovers' ardent faces
Bending to one another,
Speaking each his part.
They infinitely echo
In the red cave of my heart.
'Sweetheart, sweetheart, sweetheart,'
They said to one another.
They spoke, I think, of perils past.
They spoke, I think, of peace at last.
One thing I remember:
Spring came on forever,
Spring came on forever,"
Said the Chinese nightingale.

Vachel Lindsay

LOVE SONGS

COME [1]

Come, when the pale moon like a petal
　　Floats in the pearly dusk of Spring,
Come with arms outstretched to take me,
　　Come with lips that long to cling.

Come, for life is a frail moth flying,
　　Caught in the web of the years that pass,
And soon we two, so warm and eager,
　　Will be as the gray stones in the grass.

MESSAGE [1]

I heard a cry in the night,
　　A thousand miles it came,
Sharp as a flash of light,
　　My name, my name!

It was your voice I heard,
　　You waked and loved me so —
I send you back this word,
　　I know, I know!

MOODS [1]

I am the still rain falling,
　　Too tired for singing mirth —
Oh, be the green fields calling,
　　Oh, be for me the earth!

[1] Reprinted, by permission of the publishers, from *Love Songs*, by Sara Teasdale. Copyright, 1917, by The Macmillan Company.

I am the brown bird pining
    To leave the nest and fly —
Oh, be the fresh cloud shining,
    Oh, be for me the sky!

NIGHT SONG AT AMALFI [1]

I ASKED the heaven of stars
    What I should give my love —
It answered me with silence,
    Silence above.

I asked the darkened sea
    Down where the fishers go —
It answered me with silence,
    Silence below.

Oh, I could give him weeping,
    Or I could give him song —
But how can I give silence
    My whole life long?

SONG

LET it be forgotten as a flower is forgotten,
    Forgotten as a fire that once was singing gold,
Let it be forgotten forever and ever,
    Time is a kind friend, he will make us old.

If any one asks, say it was forgotten
    Long and long ago,
As a flower, as a fire, as a hushed footfall
    In a long forgotten snow.

Sara Teasdale

[1] Reprinted, by permission of the publishers, from *Love Songs*, by Sara Teasdale. Copyright, 1917, by the Macmillan Company.

LOVE IS A TERRIBLE THING

I WENT out to the farthest meadow,
I lay down in the deepest shadow;

And I said unto the earth, "Hold me,"
And unto the night, "O enfold me,"

And unto the wind petulantly
I cried, "You know not for you are free!"

And I begged the little leaves to lean
Low and together for a safe screen;

Then to the stars I told my tale:
"That is my home-light, there in the vale,

"And O, I know that I shall return,
But let me lie first mid the unfeeling fern.

"For there is a flame that has blown too near,
And there is a name that has grown too dear,
And there is a fear . . . "

And to the still hills and cool earth and far
     sky I made moan,
"The heart in my bosom is not my own!

"O would I were free as the wind on wing;
Love is a terrible thing!"

Grace Fallow Norton

VALLEY SONG

Your eyes and the valley are memories.
Your eyes fire and the valley a bowl.
It was here a moonrise crept over the timberline.
It was here we turned the coffee cups upside down.
And your eyes and the moon swept the valley.

I will see you again to-morrow.
I will see you again in a million years.
I will never know your dark eyes again.
These are three ghosts I keep.
These are three sumach-red dogs I run with.

All of it wraps and knots to a riddle:
I have the moon, the timberline, and you.
All three are gone — and I keep all three.

Carl Sandburg

SPRING IN CARMEL

O'er Carmel fields in the springtime the sea-gulls
    follow the plow.
  White, white wings on the blue above!
  White were your brow and breast, O Love!
    But I cannot see you now.
  Tireless ever the Mission swallow
  Dips to meadow and poppied hollow;
  Well for her mate that he can follow,
    As the buds are on the bough.

By the woods and waters of Carmel the lark is glad
    in the sun.
  Harrow! Harrow! Music of God!

Near to your nest her feet have trod
  Whose journeyings are done.
Sing, O lover! I cannot sing.
Wild and sad are the thoughts you bring.
Well for you are the skies of spring,
  And to me all skies are one.

In the beautiful woods of Carmel an iris bends
    to the wind.
O thou far-off and sorrowful flower!
Rose that I found in a tragic hour!
  Rose that I shall not find!
Petals that fell so soft and slowly,
Fragrant snows on the grasses lowly,
Gathered now would I call you holy
  Ever to eyes once blind.

In the pine-sweet valley of Carmel the cream-
    cups scatter in foam.
Azures of early lupin there!
Now the wild lilac floods the air
  Like a broken honey-comb.
So could the flowers of Paradise
Pour their souls to the morning skies;
So like a ghost your fragrance lies
  On the path that once led home.

On the emerald hills of Carmel the spring and
    winter have met.
Here I find in a gentled spot
The frost of the wild forget-me-not,
  And — I cannot forget.

Heart once light as the floating feather
Borne aloft in the sunny weather,
Spring and winter have come together —
    Shall you and she meet yet?

On the rocks and beaches of Carmel the surf is
        mighty to-day.
Breaker and lifting billow call
To the high, blue Silence over all
    With the word no heart can say.
Time-to-be, shall I hear it ever?
Time-that-is, with the hands that sever,
Cry all words but the dreadful "Never"!
    And name of her far away.

                              George Sterling

MUSIC I HEARD

Music I heard with you was more than music,
And bread I broke with you was more than bread;
Now that I am without you, all is desolate;
All that was once so beautiful is dead.

Your hands once touched this table and this silver,
And I have seen your fingers hold this glass.
These things do not remember you, belovèd, —
And yet your touch upon them will not pass.

For it was in my heart you moved among them,
And blessed them with your hands and with your eyes;
And in my heart they will remember always, —
They knew you once, O beautiful and wise.

                              Conrad Aiken

DUSK AT SEA

To-NIGHT eternity alone is near:
  The sea, the sunset, and the darkening blue;
Within their shelter is no space for fear,
  Only the wonder that such things are true.

The thought of you is like the dusk at sea —
  Space and wide freedom and old shores left far,
The shelter of a lone immensity
  Sealed by the sunset and the evening star.
                              Thomas S. Jones, Jr.

OLD SHIPS

THERE is a memory stays upon old ships,
  A weightless cargo in the musty hold, —
Of bright lagoons and prow-caressing lips,
  Of stormy midnights, — and a tale untold.
They have remembered islands in the dawn,
  And windy capes that tried their slender spars,
And tortuous channels where their keels have gone,
  And calm blue nights of stillness and the stars.

Ah, never think that ships forget a shore,
  Or bitter seas, or winds that made them wise;
There is a dream upon them, evermore; —
  And there be some who say that sunk ships rise
To seek familiar harbors in the night,
  Blowing in mists, their spectral sails like light.
                              David Morton

THE WANDERER

THE ships are lying in the bay,
  The gulls are swinging round their spars;
My soul as eagerly as they
  Desires the margin of the stars.

So much do I love wandering,
  So much I love the sea and sky,
That it will be a piteous thing
  In one small grave to lie.

                              Zoë Akins

HARBURY

ALL the men of Harbury go down to the sea in ships,
The wind upon their faces, the salt upon their lips.

The little boys of Harbury when they are laid to
    sleep,
Dream of masts and cabins and the wonders of the
    deep.

The women-folk of Harbury have eyes like the sea,
Wide with watching wonder, deep with mystery.

I met a woman: "Beyond the bar," she said,
"Beyond the shallow water where the green liner
    spread,

"Out beyond the sand-bar and the white spray,
My three sons wait for the Judgment Day."

I saw an old man who goes to sea no more,
Watch from morn till evening down on the shore.

"The sea's a hard mistress," the old man said;
"The sea is always hungry and never full fed.

"The sea had my father and took my son from me —
Sometimes I think I see them, walking on the sea!

"I'd like to be in Harbury on the Judgment Day,
When the word is spoken and the sea is wiped away,

"And all the drowned fisher boys, with sea-weed in
their hair,
Rise and walk to Harbury to greet the women there.

"I'd like to be in Harbury to see the souls arise,
Son and mother hand in hand, lovers with glad eyes.

"I think there would be many who would turn and
look with me,
Hoping for another glimpse of the cruel sea!

"They tell me that in Paradise the fields are green and
still,
With pleasant flowers everywhere that all may take
who will,

"And four great rivers flowing from out the Throne
of God
That no one ever drowns in and souls may cross dry-
shod.

"I think among those wonders there will be men like
    me,
Who miss the old salt danger of the singing sea.

"For in my heart, like some old shell, inland, safe and
    dry,
Any one who harks will still hear the sea cry."

Louise Driscoll

A LYNMOUTH WIDOW

HE was straight and strong, and his eyes were blue
As the summer meeting of sky and sea,
And the ruddy cliffs had a colder hue
Than flushed his cheek when he married me.

We passed the porch where the swallows breed,
We left the little brown church behind,
And I leaned on his arm, though I had no need,
Only to feel him so strong and kind.

One thing I never can quite forget;
It grips my throat when I try to pray —
The keen salt smell of a drying net
That hung on the churchyard wall that day.

He would have taken a long, long grave —
A long, long grave, for he stood so tall . . .
Oh, God, the crash of a breaking wave,
And the smell of the nets on the churchyard wall!

Amelia Josephine Burr

CITY ROOFS

Roof-tops, roof-tops, what do you cover?
Sad folk, bad folk, and many a glowing lover;
Wise people, simple people, children of despair —
Roof-tops, roof-tops, hiding pain and care.

Roof-tops, roof-tops, O what sin you're knowing,
While above you in the sky the white clouds are
 blowing;
While beneath you, agony and dolor and grim strife
Fight the olden battle, the olden war of Life.

Roof-tops, roof-tops, cover up their shame —
Wretched souls, prisoned souls too piteous to name;
Man himself hath built you all to hide away the
 stars —
Roof-tops roof-tops, you hide ten million scars.

Roof-tops, roof-tops, well I know you cover
Many solemn tragedies and many a lonely lover;
But ah, you hide the good that lives in the throbbing
 city —
Patient wives, and tenderness, forgiveness, faith, and
 pity.

Roof-tops, roof-tops, this is what I wonder:
You are thick as poisonous plants, thick the people
 under;
Yet roofless, and homeless, and shelterless they roam,
The driftwood of the town who have no roof-top and
 no home!

Charles Hanson Towne

EYE-WITNESS

Down by the railroad in a green valley
By dancing water, there he stayed awhile
Singing, and three men with him, listeners,
All tramps, all homeless reapers of the wind,
Motionless now and while the song went on
Transfigured into mages thronged with visions;
There with the late light of the sunset on them
And on clear water spinning from a spring
Through little cones of sand dancing and fading,
Close beside pine woods where a hermit thrush
Cast, when love dazzled him, shadows of music
That lengthened, fluting, through the singer's pauses
While the sure earth rolled eastward bringing stars
Over the singer and the men that listened
There by the roadside, understanding all.

A train went by but nothing seemed to be changed.
Some eye at a car window must have flashed
From the plush world inside the glassy Pullman,
Carelessly bearing off the scene forever,
With idle wonder what the men were doing,
Seeing they were so strangely fixed and seeing
Torn papers from their smeary dreary meal
Spread on the ground with old tomato cans
Muddy with dregs of lukewarm chicory,
Neglected while they listened to the song.
And while he sang the singer's face was lifted,
And the sky shook down a soft light upon him
Out of its branches where like fruits there were
Many beautiful stars and planets moving,
With lands upon them, rising from their seas,

Glorious lands with glittering sands upon them,
With soils of gold and magic mould for seeding,
The shining loam of lands afoam with gardens
On mightier stars with giant rains and suns
There in the heavens; but on none of all
Was there ground better than he stood upon:
There was no world there in the sky above him
Deeper in promise than the earth beneath him
Whose dust had flowered up in him the singer
And three men understanding every word.

The Tramp Sings:

I will sing, I will go, and never ask me "Why?"
I was born a rover and a passer-by.

I seem to myself like water and sky,
A river and a rover and a passer-by.

But in the winter three years back
We lit us a night fire by the track,

And the snow came up and the fire it flew
And we couldn't find the warming room for two.

One had to suffer, so I left him the fire
And I went to the weather from my heart's desire.

It was night on the line, it was no more fire,
But the zero whistle through the icy wire.

As I went suffering through the snow
Something like a shadow came moving slow.

I went up to it and I said a word;
Something flew above it like a kind of bird.

I leaned in closer and I saw a face;
A light went round me but I kept my place.

My heart went open like an apple sliced;
I saw my Saviour and I saw my Christ.

Well, you may not read it in a book,
But it takes a gentle Saviour to give a gentle look.

I looked in his eyes and I read the news;
His heart was having the railroad blues.

Oh, the railroad blues will cost you dear,
Keeps you moving on for something that you
    don't see here.

We stood and whispered in a kind of moon;
The line was looking like May and June.

I found he was a roamer and a journey man
Looking for a lodging since the night began.

He went to the doors but he did n't have the pay.
He went to the windows, then he went away.

Says, "We 'll walk together and we 'll both be fed."
Says, "I will give you the 'other' bread."

Oh, the bread he gave and without money!
O drink, O fire, O burning honey!

It went all through me like a shining storm:
I saw inside me, it was light and warm.

I saw deep under and I saw above,
I saw the stars weighed down with love.

They sang that love to burning birth,
They poured that music to the earth.

I heard the stars sing low like mothers.
He said: "Now look, and help feed others."

I looked around, and as close as touch
Was everybody that suffered much.

They reached out, there was darkness only;
They could not see us, they were lonely.

I saw the hearts that deaths took hold of,
With the wounds bare that were not told of;

Hearts with things in them making gashes;
Hearts that were choked with their dreams' ashes;

Women in front of the rolled-back air,
Looking at their breasts and nothing there;

Good men wasting and trapped in hells;
Hurt lads shivering with the fare-thee-wells.

I saw them as if something bound them;
I stood there but my heart went round them.

I begged him not to let me see them wasted.
Says, "Tell them then what you have tasted."

Told him I was weak as a rained-on bee;
Told him I was lost. — Says: "Lean on me."

Something happened then I could not tell,
But I knew I had the water for every hell.

Any other thing it was no use bringing;
They needed what the stars were singing,

What the whole sky sang like waves of light,
The tune that it danced to, day and night.

Oh, I listened to the sky for the tune to come;
The song seemed easy, but I stood there dumb.

The stars could feel me reaching through them
They let down light and drew me to them.

I stood in the sky in a light like day,
Drinking in the word that all things say

Where the worlds hang growing in clustered shapes
Dripping the music like wine from grapes.

With "Love, Love, Love," above the pain,
— The vine-like song with its wine-like rain.

Through heaven under heaven the song takes root
Of the turning, burning, deathless fruit.

I came to the earth and the pain so near me,
I tried that song but they could n't hear me.

I went down into the ground to grow,
A seed for a song that would make men know.

Into the ground from my roamer's light
I went; he watched me sink to night.

Deep in the ground from my human grieving,
His pain ploughed in me to believing.

Oh, he took earth's pain to be his bride,
While the heart of life sang in his side.

For I felt that pain, I took its kiss,
My heart broke into dust with his.

Then sudden through the earth I found life springing;
The dust men trampled on was singing.

Deep in my dust I felt its tones;
The roots of beauty went round my bones.

I stirred, I rose like a flame, like a river,
I stood on the line, I could sing forever.

Love had pierced into my human sheathing,
Song came out of me simple as breathing.

A freight came by, the line grew colder,
He laid his hand upon my shoulder.

Says, "Don't stay on the line such nights,"
And led me by the hand to the station lights.

I asked him in front of the station-house wall
If he had lodging. Says, "None at all."

I pointed to my heart and looked in his face. —
"Here, — if you have n't got a better place."

He looked and he said: "Oh, we still must roam
But if you 'll keep it open, well, I 'll call it 'home.'"

The thrush now slept whose pillow was his wing.
So the song ended and the four remained
Still in the faint starshine that silvered them,
While the low sound went on of broken water
Out of the spring and through the darkness flowing
Over a stone that held it from the sea.
Whether the men spoke after could not be told,
A mist from the ground so veiled them, but they waited
A little longer till the moon came up;
Then on the gilded track leading to the mountains,
Against the moon they faded in common gold
And earth bore East with all toward the new morning.

Ridgely Torrence

GOD'S ACRE

BECAUSE we felt there could not be
A mowing in reality
So white and feathery-blown and gay
With blossoms of wild caraway,
I said to Celia, "Let us trace
The secret of this pleasant place!"

We knew some deeper beauty lay
Below the bloom of caraway,
And when we bent the white aside
We came to paupers who had died:
Rough wooden shingles row on row,
And God's name written there — *John Doe.*
                              Witter Bynner

GENERAL WILLIAM BOOTH ENTERS
INTO HEAVEN [1]

(To be sung to the tune of *The Blood of the Lamb* with
indicated instrument)

I

(Bass drum beaten loudly)

BOOTH led boldly with his big bass drum —
(Are you washed in the blood of the Lamb?)
The Saints smiled gravely and they said: "He's come."
(Are you washed in the blood of the Lamb?)
Walking lepers followed, rank on rank,
Lurching bravoes from the ditches dank,
Drabs from the alleyways and drug fiends pale —
Minds still passion-ridden, soul-powers frail: —
Vermin-eaten saints with mouldy breath,
Unwashed legions with the ways of Death —
(Are you washed in the blood of the Lamb?)

(Banjos)

Every slum had sent its half-a-score
The round world over. (Booth had groaned for more.)
Every banner that the wide world flies
Bloomed with glory and transcendent dyes.

[1] Reprinted, by permission of the publishers, from *General William Booth
Enters into Heaven, and Other Poems*, by Vachel Lindsay. Copyright, 1913,
by The Macmillan Company.

Big-voiced lasses made their banjos bang,
Tranced, fanatical, they shrieked and sang: —
"Are you washed in the blood of the Lamb?"
Hallelujah! It was queer to see
Bull-necked convicts with that land make free.
Loons with trumpets blowed a blare, blare, blare,
On, on upward thro' the golden air!
(Are you washed in the blood of the Lamb?)

II

(Bass drum slower and softer)

Booth died blind and still by Faith he trod,
Eyes still dazzled by the ways of God.
Booth led boldly, and he looked the chief,
Eagle countenance in sharp relief,
Beard a-flying, air of high command
Unabated in that holy land.

(Sweet flute music)

Jesus came from out the court-house door,
Stretched his hands above the passing poor.
Booth saw not, but led his queer ones there
Round and round the mighty court-house square.
Yet in an instant all that blear review
Marched on spotless, clad in raiment new.
The lame were straightened, withered limbs uncurled
And blind eyes opened on a new, sweet world.

(Bass drum louder)

Drabs and vixens in a flash made whole!
Gone was the weasel-head, the snout, the jowl!
Sages and sibyls now, and athletes clean,
Rulers of empires and of forests green!

(*Grand chorus of all instruments. Tambourines to the
foreground*)

The hosts were sandalled, and their wings were
  fire!
(Are you washed in the blood of the Lamb?)
But their noise played havoc with the angel-choir
(Are you washed in the blood of the Lamb?)
O, shout Salvation! It was good to see
Kings and Princes by the Lamb set free.
The banjos rattled and the tambourines
Jing-jing-jingled in the hands of Queens.

(*Reverently sung, no instruments*)

And when Booth halted by the curb for prayer
He saw his Master thro' the flag-filled air.
Christ came gently with a robe and crown
For Booth the soldier, while the throng knelt down.
He saw King Jesus. They were face to face,
And he knelt a-weeping in that holy place.
Are you washed in the blood of the Lamb?
        Vachel Lindsay

COMPENSATION

I KNOW the sorrows of the last abyss:
I walked the cold black pools without a star;
I lay on rock of unseen flint and spar;
I heard the execrable serpent hiss;
I dreamed of sun, fruit-tree, and virgin's kiss;
I woke alone with midnight near and far,
And everlasting hunger, keen to mar;
But I arose, and my reward is this:

I am no more one more amid the throng:
Though name be naught, and lips forever weak,
I seem to know at last of mighty song;
And with no blush, no tremor on the cheek,
I do claim consort with the great and strong
Who suffered ill and had the gift to speak.

William Ellery Leonard

A GIRL'S SONGS

BORROWER

I SING of sorrow,
　　I sing of weeping.
I have no sorrow.

I only borrow
From some tomorrow
　　Where it lies sleeping,
Enough of sorrow
　　To sing of weeping.

VINTAGE

Heartbreak that is too new
　　Can not be used to make
Beauty that will startle;
　　That takes an old heartbreak.

Old heartbreaks are old wine.
Too new to pour is mine.

THE KISS

Your kiss lies on my face
　　Like the first snow
Upon a summer place.

Bewildered by that wonder,
The grasses tremble under
The thing they do not know.
I tremble even so.

FREE

Over and over
 I tell the sky:
 I am free — I!

Over and over I tell the sea:
 — I am free!

Over and over I tell my lover
 I am free, free!
Over and over.

But when the night comes black and cold,
I who am young, with fear grow old;
And I know, when the world is clear of sound,
I am bound — bound.
     Mary Carolyn Davies

THE ENCHANTED SHEEPFOLD

THE hills far-off were blue, blue,
 The hills at hand were brown;
And all the herd-bells called to me
 As I came by the down.

The briars turned to roses, roses,
 Ever we stayed to pull

A white little rose, and a red little rose,
    And a lock of silver wool.

Nobody heeded,— none, none;
    And when True Love came by,
They thought him naught but the shepherd-boy.
    Nobody knew but I!

The trees were feathered like birds, birds;
    Birds were in every tree.
Yet nobody heeded, nobody heard,
    Nobody knew, save me.

And he is fairer than all — all.
    How could a heart go wrong?
For his eyes I knew, and his knew mine,
    Like an old, old song.

                    Josephine Preston Peabody

WHERE LOVE IS

By the rosy cliffs of Devon, on a green hill's crest,
I would build me a house as a swallow builds its nest;
I would curtain it with roses, and the wind should
        breathe to me
The sweetness of the roses and the saltness of the sea.

Where the Tuscan olives whiten in the hot blue day,
I would hide me from the heat in a little hut of gray,
While the singing of the husbandman should scale my
        lattice green
From the golden rows of barley that the poppies blaze
        between.

Narrow is the street, Dear, and dingy are the walls
Wherein I wait your coming as the twilight falls.
All day with dreams I gild the grime till at your step
    I start —
Ah Love, my country in your arms — my home upon
    your heart!
                     Amelia Josephine Burr

INTERLUDE [1]

I AM not old, but old enough
To know that you are very young.
It might be said I am the leaf,
And you the blossom newly sprung.

So I shall grow a while with you,
And hear the bee and watch the cloud,
Before the dragon on the branch,
The caterpillar, weaves a shroud.
                     Scudder Middleton

THE LOVER ENVIES AN OLD MAN

I ENVY the feeble old man
Dozing there in the sun.
When all you can do is done
And life is a shattered plan,
What is there better than
Dozing in the sun?

I could grow very still
Like an old stone on a hill

[1] Reprinted, by permission of the publishers, from *The New Day*, by Scudder Middleton. Copyright, 1919, by The Macmillan Company.

And content me with the one
Thing that is ever kind,
The tender sun.
I could grow deaf and blind
And never hear her voice,
Nor think I could rejoice
With her in any place;
And I could forget her face,
And love only the sun.
Because when we are tired,
Very very tired,
And cannot again be fired
By any hope,
The sun is so comforting!
A little bird under the wing
Of its mother, is not so warm.
Give me only the scope
Of an old chair
Out in the air,
Let me rest there,
Moving not,
Loving not,
Only dozing my days till my days be done,
Under the sun.

Shaemas O Sheel

IF YOU SHOULD TIRE OF LOVING ME

If you should tire of loving me
  Some one of our far days,
Oh, never start to hide your heart
  Or cover thought with praise.

For every word you would not say
    Be sure my heart has heard,
So go from me all silently
    Without a kiss or word;

For God must give you happiness,
    And Oh, it may befall
In listening long to Heaven-song
    I may not care at all!

Margaret Widdemer

THE FLOWER OF MENDING [1]

WHEN Dragon-fly would fix his wings,
When Snail would patch his house,
When moths have marred the overcoat
Of tender Mister Mouse,

The pretty creatures go with haste
To the sunlit blue-grass hills
Where the Flower of Mending yields the wax
And webs to help their ills.

The hour the coats are waxed and webbed
They fall into a dream,
And when they wake the ragged robes
Are joined without a seam.

My heart is but a dragon-fly,
My heart is but a mouse,
My heart is but a haughty snail
In a little stony house.

[1] Reprinted, by permission of the publishers, from *The Chinese Nightingale, and Other Poems*, by Vachel Lindsay. Copyright, 1917, by The Macmillan Company.

Your hand was honey-comb to heal,
Your voice a web to bind.
You were a Mending Flower to me
To cure my heart and mind.

Vachel Lindsay

VENUS TRANSIENS [1]

TELL me,
Was Venus more beautiful
Than you are,
When she topped
The crinkled waves,
Drifting shoreward
On her plaited shell?
Was Botticelli's vision
Fairer than mine;
And were the painted rosebuds
He tossed his lady,
Of better worth
Than the words I blow about you
To cover your too great loveliness
As with a gauze
Of misted silver?

For me,
You stand poised
In the blue and buoyant air,
Cinctured by bright winds,
Treading the sunlight.
And the waves which precede you
Ripple and stir
The sands at your feet.

Amy Lowell

[1] Reprinted, by permission of the publishers, from *Pictures of the Floating World*, by Amy Lowell. Copyright. 1919, by The Macmillan Company.

THE DREAM OF AENGUS OG

WHEN the rose of Morn through the Dawn was breaking.
  And white on the hearth was last night's flame,
Thither to me 'twixt sleeping and waking,
  Singing out of the mists she came.

And grey as the mists on the spectre meadows
  Were the eyes that on my eyes she laid,
And her hair's red splendor through the shadows
  Like to the marsh-fire gleamed and played.

And she sang of the wondrous far-off places
  That a man may only see in dreams,
The death-still, odorous, starlit spaces
  Where Time is lost and no life gleams.

And there till the day had its crest uplifted,
  She stood with her still face bent on me,
Then forth with the Dawn departing drifted
  Light as a foam-fleck on the sea.

And now my heart is the heart of a swallow
  That here no solace of rest may find,
Forevermore I follow and follow
  Her white feet glancing down the wind.

And forevermore in my ears are ringing —
  (Oh, red lips yet shall I kiss you dumb!)
Twain sole words of that May morn's singing,
  Calling to me "Hither"! and "Come"!

From flower-bright fields to the wild lake-sedges
  Crying my steps when the Day has gone,

Till dim and small down the Night's pale edges
   The stars have fluttered one by one.

And light as the thought of a love forgotten,
   The hours skim past, while before me flies
That face of the Sun and Mist begotten,
   Its singing lips and death-cold eyes.

Eleanor Rogers Cox

"I AM IN LOVE WITH HIGH FAR-SEEING PLACES"

I AM in love with high far-seeing places
That look on plains half-sunlight and half-storm, —
In love with hours when from the circling faces
Veils pass, and laughing fellowship glows warm.
You who look on me with grave eyes where rapture
And April love of living burn confessed,—
The Gods are good! The world lies free to capture!
Life has no walls. O take me to your breast!
Take me, — be with me for a moment's span! —
I am in love with all unveilèd faces.
I seek the wonder at the heart of man;
I would go up to the far-seeing places.
While youth is ours, turn toward me for a space
The marvel of your rapture-lighted face!

Arthur Davison Ficke

YOU

   DEEP in the heart of me,
   Nothing but You!
   See through the art of me —
   Deep in the heart of me

Find the best part of me,
Changeless and true.
Deep in the heart of me,
Nothing but You!

Ruth Guthrie Harding

CHOICE

I'd rather have the thought of you
To hold against my heart,
My spirit to be taught of you
With west winds blowing,
Than all the warm caresses
Of another love's bestowing,
Or all the glories of the world
In which you had no part.

I'd rather have the theme of you
To thread my nights and days,
I'd rather have the dream of you
With faint stars glowing,
I'd rather have the want of you,
The rich, elusive taunt of you
Forever and forever and forever unconfessed
Than claim the alien comfort
Of any other's breast.

O lover! O my lover,
That this should come to me!
I'd rather have the hope for you,
Ah, Love, I'd rather grope for you
Within the great abyss
Than claim another's kiss —

Alone I'd rather go my way
Throughout eternity.

Angela Morgan

SONG

THE bride, she wears a white, white rose — the
    plucking it was mine;
The poet wears a laurel wreath — and I the laurel
    twine;
And oh, the child, your little child, that's clinging
    close to you,
It laughs to wear my violets — they are so sweet and
    blue!

And I, I have a wreath to wear — ah, never rue nor
    thorn!
I sometimes think that bitter wreath could be more
    sweetly worn!
For mine is made of ghostly bloom, of what I can't
    forget —
The fallen leaves of other crowns — rose, laurel,
    violet!

Margaret Steele Anderson

ROMANCE [1]

WHY should we argue with the falling dust
Or tremble in the traffic of the days?
Our hearts are music-makers in the clouds,
Our feet are running on the heavenly ways.

[1] Reprinted, by permission of the publishers, from *The New Day*, by
Scudder Middleton.   Copyright, 1919, by The Macmillan Company.

We'll go and find the honey of romance
Within the hollow of the sacred tree.
There is a spirit in the eastern sky,
Calling along the dawn to you and me.

She'll lead us to the forest where she hides
The yellow wine that keeps the angels young —
We are the chosen lovers of the earth
For whom alone the golden comb was hung.

Scudder Middleton

GOOD-BYE

Good-bye to tree and tower,
To meadow, stream, and hill,
Beneath the white clouds marshalled close
At the wind's will.

Good-bye to the gay garden,
With prim geraniums pied,
And spreading yew trees, old, unchanging
Tho' men have died.

Good-bye to the New Castle,
With granite walls and grey,
And rooms where faded greatness still
Lingers to-day.

To every friend in Mallow,
When I am gone afar,
These words of ancient Celtic hope,
"Peace after war."

I would return to Erin
When all these wars are by,
Live long among her hills before
My last good-bye.

Norreys Jephson O'Conor

BEYOND RATHKELLY

As I went over the Far Hill,
    Just beyond Rathkelly,
    — Och, to be on the Far Hill
    O'er Newtonstewart Town!
As I went over the Far Hill
    With Marget's daughter Nellie,
The night was up and the moon was out,
    And a star was falling down.

As I went over the Far Hill,
    Just beyond Rathkelly,
    — Och, to be on the Far Hill
    Above the Bridge o'Moyle!
As I went over the Far Hill,
    With Marget's daughter Nellie,
I made a wish before the star
    Had fallen in the Foyle.

As I went over the Far Hill,
    Just beyond Rathkelly,
    — Och, to be on the Far Hill
    With the hopes that I had then!
As I went over the Far Hill,
    I wished for little Nellie,
And if a star were falling now
    I'd wish for her again.

Francis Carlin

A SONG OF TWO WANDERERS

DEAR, when I went with you
To where the town ends,
Simple things that Christ loved —
They were our friends;
Tree shade and grass blade
And meadows in flower;
Sun-sparkle, dew-glisten,
Star-glow and shower;
Cool-flowing song at night
Where the river bends,
And the shingle croons a tune —
These were our friends.

Under us the brown earth
Ancient and strong,
The best bed for wanderers
All the night long;
Over us the blue sky
Ancient and dear,
The best roof to shelter all
Glad wanderers here;
And racing between them there
Falls and ascends
The chantey of the clean winds —
These were our friends.

By day on the broad road
Or on the narrow trail,
Angel wings shadowed us,
Glimmering pale

Through the red heat of noon;
In the twilight of dawn
Fairies broke fast with us;
Prophets led us on,
Heroes were kind to us
Day after happy day;
Many white Madonnas
We met on our way —
Farmer and longshoreman,
Fisherman and wife,
Children and laborers
Brave enough for Life,
Simple folk that Christ loved —
They were our friends. . . .

Dear, we must go again
To where the town ends. . .
                    Marguerite Wilkinson

IN THE MUSHROOM MEADOWS

SUN on the dewy grasslands where late the frost hath
        shone,
And lo, what elfin cities are these we come upon!
What pigmy domes and thatches, what Arab caravan,
What downy-roofed pagodas that have known no
        touch of man!
Are these the oldtime meadows? Yes, the wildgrape
        scents the air;
The breath of ripened orchards still is incense every-
        where;
Yet do these dawn-encampments bring the lurking
        memories
Of Egypt and of Burma and the shores of China Seas.
                    Thomas Walsh

THE PATH THAT LEADS TO NOWHERE

There's a path that leads to Nowhere
   In a meadow that I know,
Where an inland island rises
   And the stream is still and slow;
There it wanders under willows
   And beneath the silver green
Of the birches' silent shadows
   Where the early violets lean.

Other pathways lead to Somewhere,
   But the one I love so well
Had no end and no beginning —
   Just the beauty of the dell,
Just the windflowers and the lilies
   Yellow striped as adder's tongue,
Seem to satisfy my pathway
   As it winds their sweets among.

There I go to meet the Springtime,
   When the meadow is aglow,
Marigolds amid the marshes, —
   And the stream is still and slow. —
There I find my fair oasis,
   And with care-free feet I tread
For the pathway leads to Nowhere,
   And the blue is overhead!

All the ways that lead to Somewhere
   Echo with the hurrying feet
Of the Struggling and the Striving,
   But the way I find so sweet

Bids me dream and bids me linger,
Joy and Beauty are its goal, —
On the path that leads to Nowhere
I have sometimes found my soul!

Corinne Roosevelt Robinson

DAYS

SOME days my thoughts are just cocoons — all cold,
and dull, and blind,
They hang from dripping branches in the grey woods
of my mind;

And other days they drift and shine — such free and
flying things!
I find the gold-dust in my hair, left by their brushing
wings.

Karle Wilson Baker

ELLIS PARK

LITTLE park that I pass through,
I carry off a piece of you
Every morning hurrying down
To my work-day in the town;
Carry you for country there
To make the city ways more fair.
I take your trees,
And your breeze,
Your greenness,
Your cleanness,
Some of your shade, some of your sky,
Some of your calm as I go by;

Your flowers to trim
The pavements grim;
Your space for room in the jostled street
And grass for carpet to my feet.
Your fountains take and sweet bird calls
To sing me from my office walls.
All that I can see
I carry off with me.
But you never miss my theft,
So much treasure you have left.
As I find you, fresh at morning,
So I find you, home returning —
Nothing lacking from your grace.
All your riches wait in place
For me to borrow
On the morrow.

Do you hear this praise of you,
Little park that I pass through?

Helen Hoyt

A NOTE FROM THE PIPES

PAN, blow your pipes and I will be
Your fern, your pool, your dream, your tree!

I heard you play, caught your swift eye,
"A pretty melody!" called I,
"Hail, Pan!" And sought to pass you by.

Now blow your pipes and I will sing
To your sure lips' accompanying!

Wild God, who lifted me from earth,
Who taught me freedom, wisdom, mirth,
Immortalized my body's worth, —

Blow, blow your pipes! And from afar
I 'll come — I 'll be your bird, your star,
Your wood, your nymph, your kiss, your rhyme,
And all your godlike summer-time!

Leonora Speyer

AFTERNOON ON A HILL

I WILL be the gladdest thing
    Under the sun!
I will touch a hundred flowers
    And not pick one.

I will look at cliffs and clouds
    With quiet eyes,
Watch the wind bow down the grass,
    And the grass rise.

And when lights begin to show
    Up from the town,
I will mark which must be mine,
    And then start down!

Edna St. Vincent Millay

OPEN WINDOWS

OUT of the window a sea of green trees
    Lift their soft boughs like the arms of a dancer;
They beckon and call me, "Come out in the sun!"
    But I cannot answer.

I am alone with Weakness and Pain,
  Sick abed and June is going,
I cannot keep her, she hurries by
  With the silver-green of her garments blowing.

Men and women pass in the street
  Glad of the shining sapphire weather;
But we know more of it than they,
  Pain and I together.

They are the runners in the sun,
  Breathless and blinded by the race,
But we are watchers in the shade
  Who speak with Wonder face to face.

                                  Sara Teasdale

OLD AMAZE

MINE eyes are filled today with old amaze
  At mountains, and at meadows deftly strewn
  With bits of the gay jewelry of June
And of her splendid vesture; and, agaze,
I stand where Spring her bright brocade of days
  Embroidered o'er, and listen to the flow
  Of sudden runlets — the faint blasts they blow,
Low, on their stony bugles, in still ways.
For wonders are at one, confederate yet:
  Yea, where the wearied year came to a close,
  An odor reminiscent of the rose;
And everywhere her seal has Summer set;
  And, as of old, in the horizon-sky,
  The sun can find a lovely place to die.

                              Mahlon Leonard Fisher

VOYAGE À L'INFINI

THE swan existing
Is like a song with an accompaniment
Imaginary.

Across the grassy lake,
Across the lake to the shadow of the willows,
It is accompanied by an image,
— as by Debussy's
"Reflets dans l'eau."

The swan that is
Reflects
Upon the solitary water — breast to breast
With the duplicity:
"*The other one!*"

And breast to breast it is confused.
O visionary wedding! O stateliness of the procession
It is accompanied by the image of itself
Alone.

At night
The lake is a wide silence,
Without imagination.

Walter Conrad Arensberg

AFTER SUNSET

I HAVE an understanding with the hills
At evening when the slanted radiance fills
Their hollows, and the great winds let them be,
And they are quiet and look down at me.

Oh, then I see the patience in their eyes
Out of the centuries that made them wise.
They lend me hoarded memory and I learn
Their thoughts of granite and their whims of fern,
And why a dream of forests must endure
Though every tree be slain: and how the pure,
Invisible beauty has a word so brief
A flower can say it or a shaken leaf,
But few may ever snare it in a song,
Though for the quest a life is not too long.
When the blue hills grow tender, when they pull
The twilight close with gesture beautiful,
And shadows are their garments, and the air
Deepens, and the wild veery is at prayer, —
Their arms are strong around me; and I know
That somehow I shall follow when you go
To the still land beyond the evening star,
Where everlasting hills and valleys are:
And silence may not hurt us any more,
And terror shall be past, and grief, and war.

Grace Hazard Conkling

MORNING SONG OF SENLIN

It is morning, Senlin says, and in the morning
When the light drips through the shutters like the
    dew,
I arise, I face the sunrise,
And do the things my fathers learned to do.
Stars in the purple dusk above the rooftops
Pale in a saffron mist and seem to die,
And I myself on a swiftly tilting planet
Stand before a glass and tie my tie.

Vine leaves tap my window,
Dew-drops sing to the garden stones,
The robin chirps in the chinaberry tree
Repeating three clear tones.

It is morning. I stand by the mirror
And tie my tie once more.
While waves far off in a pale rose twilight
Crash on a white sand shore.
I stand by a mirror and comb my hair:
How small and white my face! —
The green earth tilts through a sphere of air
And bathes in a flame of space.
There are houses hanging above the stars
And stars hung under a sea . . .
And a sun far off in a shell of silence
Dapples my walls for me . . .

It is morning, Senlin says, and in the morning
Should I not pause in the light to remember God?
Upright and firm I stand on a star unstable,
He is immense and lonely as a cloud.
I will dedicate this moment before my mirror
To him alone, for him I will comb my hair.
Accept these humble offerings, cloud of silence!
I will think of you as I descend the stair.

Vine leaves tap my window,
The snail-track shines on the stones,
Dew-drops flash from the chinaberry tree
Repeating two clear tones.

It is morning, I awake from a bed of silence,
Shining I rise from the starless waters of sleep.

The walls are about me still as in the evening,
I am the same, and the same name still I keep.
The earth revolves with me, yet makes no motion,
The stars pale silently in a coral sky.
In a whistling void I stand before my mirror,
Unconcerned, and tie my tie.

There are horses neighing on far-off hills
Tossing their long white manes,
And mountains flash in the rose-white dusk,
Their shoulders black with rains . . .
It is morning. I stand by the mirror
And surprise my soul once more;
The blue air rushes above my ceiling,
There are suns beneath my floor . . .

. . . It is morning, Senlin says, I ascend from darkness
And depart on the winds of space for I know not where,
My watch is wound, a key is in my pocket,
And the sky is darkened as I descend the stair.
There are shadows across the windows, clouds in heaven,
And a god among the stars; and I will go
Thinking of him as I might think of daybreak
And humming a tune I know . . .

Vine-leaves tap at the window,
Dew-drops sing to the garden stones,
The robin chirps in the chinaberry tree
Repeating three clear tones.

Conrad Aiken

GOOD COMPANY

To-day I have grown taller from walking with the trees,
  The seven sister-poplars who go softly in a line;
And I think my heart is whiter for its parley with a star
  That trembled out at nightfall and hung above the pine.

The call-note of a redbird from the cedars in the dusk
  Woke his happy mate within me to an answer free
      and fine;
And a sudden angel beckoned from a column of blue
      smoke —
  Lord, who am I that they should stoop — these holy folk
      of thine?

                                        Karle Wilson Baker

"FEUERZAUBER"

I never knew the earth had so much gold —
  The fields run over with it, and this hill,
Hoary and old,
  Is young with buoyant blooms that flame and thrill.

Such golden fires, such yellow — lo, how good
  This spendthrift world, and what a lavish God —
This fringe of wood,
  Blazing with buttercup and goldenrod.

You too, beloved, are changed. Again I see
  Your face grow mystical, as on that night
You turned to me,
  And all the trembling world — and you — were
      white.

Aye, you are touched; your singing lips grow dumb;
  The fields absorb you, color you entire . . .
And you become
  A goddess standing in a world of fire!

Louis Untermeyer

BIRCHES

WHEN I see birches bend to left and right
Across the lines of straighter darker trees,
I like to think some boy's been swinging them.
But swinging does n't bend them down to stay.
Ice-storms do that. Often you must have seen them
Loaded with ice a sunny winter morning
After a rain. They click upon themselves
As the breeze rises, and turn many-colored
As the stir cracks and crazes their enamel.
Soon the sun's warmth makes them shed crystal shells,
Shattering and avalanching on the snow-crust —
Such heaps of broken glass to sweep away
You 'd think the inner dome of heaven had fallen.
They are dragged to the withered bracken by the load,
And they seem not to break; though once they are
          bowed
So low for long, they never right themselves:
You may see their trunks arching in the woods
Years afterwards, trailing their leaves on the ground
Like girls on hands and knees that throw their hair
Before them over their heads to dry in the sun.
But I was going to say when Truth broke in
With all her matter-of-fact about the ice-storm
(Now am I free to be poetical?)
I should prefer to have some boy bend them

As he went out and in to fetch the cows —
Some boy too far from town to learn baseball,
Whose only play was what he found himself,
Summer or winter, and could play alone.
One by one he subdued his father's trees
By riding them down over and over again
Until he took the stiffness out of them,
And not one but hung limp, not one was left
For him to conquer. He learned all there was
To learn about not launching out too soon
And so not carrying the tree away
Clear to the ground. He always kept his poise
To the top branches, climbing carefully
With the same pains you use to fill a cup
Up to the brim, and even above the brim.
Then he flung outward, feet first, with a swish,
Kicking his way down through the air to the ground.
So was I once myself a swinger of birches.
And so I dream of going back to be.
It's when I'm weary of considerations,
And life is too much like a pathless wood
Where your face burns and tickles with the cobwebs
Broken across it, and one eye is weeping
From a twig's having lashed across it open.
I'd like to get away from earth awhile
And then come back to it and begin over.
May no fate willfully misunderstand me
And half grant what I wish and snatch me away
Not to return. Earth's the right place for love:
I don't know where it's likely to go better.
I'd like to go by climbing a birch tree,
And climb black branches up a snow-white trunk
Toward heaven, till the tree could bear no more,

But dipped its top and set me down again.
That would be good both going and coming back.
One could do worse than be a swinger of birches.
                                        Robert Frost

FIFTY YEARS SPENT

FIFTY years spent before I found me,
Wind on my mouth and the taste of the rain,
Where the great hills circled and swept around me
And the torrents leapt to the mist-drenched plain;
Ah, it was long this coming of me
Back to the hills and the sounding sea.

Ye who can go when so it tideth
To fallow fields when the Spring is new,
Finding the spirit that there abideth,
Taking fill of the sun and the dew;
Little ye know of the cross of the town
And the small pale folk who go up and down.

Fifty years spent before I found me
A bank knee-deep with climbing rose,
Saw, or had space to look around me,
Knew how the apple buds and blows;
And all the while that I thought me wise
I walked as one with blinded eyes.

Scarcely a lad who passes twenty
But finds him a girl to balm his heart;
Only I, who had work so plenty,
Bade this loving keep apart:
Once I saw a girl in a crowd,
But I hushed my heart when it cried out aloud.

City courts in January, —
City courts in wilted June,
Often ye will catch and carry
Echoes of some straying tune:
Ah, but underneath the feet
Echo stifles in a street.

Fifty years spent, and what do they bring me?
Now I can buy the meadow and hill:
Where is the heart of the boy to sing thee?
Where is the life for thy living to fill?
And thirty years back in a city crowd
I passed a girl when my heart cried loud!

Maxwell Struthers Burt

THE CITY

WHEN, sick of all the sorrow and distress
    That flourished in the City like foul weeds,
    I sought blue rivers and green, opulent meads,
And leagues of unregarded loneliness
Whereon no foot of man had seemed to press,
    I did not know how great had been my needs,
    How wise the woodland's gospels and her creeds,
How good her faith to one long comfortless.

But in the silence came a Voice to me;
    In every wind it murmured, and I knew
        It would not cease though far my heart might roam.
It called me in the sunrise and the dew,
    At noon and twilight, sadly, hungrily,
        The jealous City, whispering always — "Home!"

Charles Hanson Towne

THE MOST-SACRED MOUNTAIN

Space, and the twelve clean winds of heaven,
And this sharp exultation, like a cry, after the slow
    six thousand steps of climbing!
This is Tai Shan, the beautiful, the most holy.

Below my feet the foot-hills nestle, brown with flecks
    of green; and lower down the flat brown plain,
    the floor of earth, stretches away to blue in-
    finity.
Beside me in this airy space the temple roofs cut their
    slow curves against the sky,
And one black bird circles above the void.

Space, and the twelve clean winds are here;
And with them broods eternity — a swift, white peace,
    a presence manifest.
The rhythm ceases here. Time has no place. This is
    the end that has no end.

Here, when Confucius came, a half a thousand years
    before the Nazarene, he stepped, with me, thus
    into timelessness.
The stone beside us waxes old, the carven stone that
    says: "On this spot once Confucius stood and
    felt the smallness of the world below."
The stone grows old:
Eternity is not for stones.
But I shall go down from this airy place, this swift
    white peace, this stinging exultation.

And time will close about me, and my soul stir to the
  rhythm of the daily round.
Yet, having known, life will not press so close,
  and always I shall feel time ravel thin about me;
For once I stood
In the white windy presence of eternity.

        Eunice Tietjens

THE CHANT OF THE COLORADO

(At the Grand Canyon)

My brother, man, shapes him a plan
  And builds him a house in a day,
But I have toiled through a million years
  For a home to last alway.
I have flooded the sands and washed them
    down,
  I have cut through gneiss and granite.
No toiler of earth has wrought as I,
  Since God's first breath began it.
High mountain-buttes I have chiselled, to
    shade
  My wanderings to the sea.
With the wind's aid, and the cloud's aid,
Unweary and mighty and unafraid,
  I have bodied eternity.

My brother, man, builds for a span:
  His life is a moment's breath.
But I have hewn for a million years,
  Nor a moment dreamt of death.
By moons and stars I have measured my task —
  And some from the skies have perished:

But ever I cut and flashed and foamed,
  As ever my aim I cherished:
My aim to quarry the heart of earth,
  Till, in the rock's red rise,
Its age and birth, through an awful girth
Of strata, should show the wonder-worth
  Of patience to all eyes.

My brother, man, builds as he can,
  And beauty he adds for his joy,
But all the hues of sublimity
  My pinnacled walls employ.
Slow shadows iris them all day long,
  And silvery veils, soul-stilling,
The moon drops down their precipices,
  Soft with a spectral thrilling.
For all immutable dreams that sway
  With beauty the earth and air,
Are ever at play, by night and day,
My house of eternity to array
  In visions ever fair.

Cale Young Rice

THE WATER OUZEL

LITTLE brown surf-bather of the mountains!
Spirit of foam, lover of cataracts, shaking your wings
    in falling waters!
Have you no fear of the roar and rush when Nevada
    plunges —
Nevada, the shapely dancer, feeling her way with slim
    white fingers?

How dare you dash at Yosemite the mighty —
Tall, white limbed Yosemite, leaping down, down over
      the cliff?
Is it not enough to lean on the blue air of moun-
      tains?
Is it not enough to rest with your mate at timberline,
      in bushes that hug the rocks?
Must you fly through mad waters where the heaped-up
      granite breaks them?
Must you batter your wings in the torrent?
Must you plunge for life and death through the foam?

Harriet Monroe

OLD MANUSCRIPT

THE sky
Is that beautiful old parchment
In which the sun
And the moon
Keep their diary.
To read it all,
One must be a linguist
More learned than Father Wisdom;
And a visionary
More clairvoyant than Mother Dream.
But to feel it,
One must be an apostle:
One who is more than intimate
In having been, always,
The only confidant —
Like the earth
Or the sky.

Alfred Kreymborg

THE RUNNER IN THE SKIES

Who is the runner in the skies,
With her blowing scarf of stars,
And our Earth and sun hovering like bees about her
    blossoming heart?
Her feet are on the winds, where space is deep,
Her eyes are nebulous and veiled,
She hurries through the night to a far lover.

James Oppenheim

EVENING SONG OF SENLIN

It is moonlight. Alone in the silence
I ascend my stairs once more,
While waves, remote in a pale blue starlight,
Crash on a white sand shore.
It is moonlight. The garden is silent.
I stand in my room alone.
Across my wall, from the far-off moon,
A rain of fire is thrown . . .

There are houses hanging above the stars,
And stars hung under a sea:
And a wind from the long blue vault of time
Waves my curtains for me . . .

I wait in the dark once more,
Swung between space and space:
Before my mirror I lift my hands
And face my remembered face.
Is it I who stand in a question here,
Asking to know my name? . . .

It is I, yet I know not whither I go,
Nor why, nor whence I came.

It is I, who awoke at dawn
And arose and descended the stair,
Conceiving a god in the eye of the sun, —
In a woman's hands and hair.
It is I whose flesh is grey with the stones
I builded into a wall:
With a mournful melody in my brain
Of a tune I cannot recall . . .

There are roses to kiss: and mouths to kiss;
And the sharp-pained shadow of death.
I remember a rain-drop on my cheek, —
A wind like a fragrant breath . . .
And the star I laugh on tilts through heaven;
And the heavens are dark and steep . . .
I will forget these things once more
In the silence of sleep.

Conrad Aiken

A THRUSH IN THE MOONLIGHT

IN came the moon and covered me with wonder,
Touched me and was near me and made me very still.
In came a rush of song, like rain after thunder,
Pouring importunate on my window-sill.

I lowered my head, I hid it, I would not see nor hear,
The birdsong had stricken me, had brought the moon
      too near.

But when I dared to lift my head, night began to
   fill
With singing in the darkness. And then the thrush
   grew still.
   And the moon came in, and silence, on my window-
      sill.

Witter Bynner

ORCHARD

I saw the first pear
As it fell —
The honey-seeking, golden-banded,
The yellow swarm
Was not more fleet than I,
(Spare us from loveliness)
And I fell prostrate
Crying:
You have flayed us
With your blossoms,
Spare us the beauty
Of fruit-trees.

The honey-seeking
Paused not,
The air thundered their song,
And I alone was prostrate.

O rough-hewn
God of the orchard,
I bring you an offering —
Do you, alone unbeautiful,

Son of the god,
Spare us from loveliness:

These fallen hazel-nuts,
Stripped late of their green sheaths,
Grapes, red-purple,
Their berries
Dripping with wine,
Pomegranates already broken,
And shrunken figs
And quinces untouched,
I bring you as offering.

H. D.

HEAT

O wind, rend open the heat,
Cut apart the heat,
Rend it to tatters.

Fruit cannot drop
Through this thick air —
Fruit cannot fall into heat
That presses up and blunts
The points of pears
And rounds the grapes.

Cut the heat —
Plough through it,
Turning it on either side
Of your path.

H. D.

MADONNA OF THE EVENING FLOWERS [1]

ALL day long I have been working,
Now I am tired.
I call: "Where are you?"
But there is only the oak tree rustling in the wind.
The house is very quiet,
The sun shines in on your books,
On your scissors and thimble just put down,
But you are not there.
Suddenly I am lonely:
Where are you?
I go about searching.

Then I see you,
Standing under a spire of pale blue larkspur,
With a basket of roses on your arm.
You are cool, like silver,
And you smile.
I think the Canterbury bells are playing little tunes.

You tell me that the peonies need spraying,
That the columbines have overrun all bounds,
That the pyrus japonica should be cut back and
        rounded.
You tell me these things.
But I look at you, heart of silver,
White heart-flame of polished silver,
Burning beneath the blue steeples of the larkspur.
And I long to kneel instantly at your feet,
While all about us peal the loud, sweet *Te Deums* of the
        Canterbury bells.

Amy Lowell

[1] Reprinted, by permission of the publishers, from *Pictures of the Float ing World*, by Amy Lowell. Copyright, 1919, by The Macmillan Company

THE NEW GOD

YE morning-glories, ring in the gale your bells,
And with dew water the walk's dust for the burden-
      bearing ants:
Ye swinging spears of the larkspur, open your wells of
      gold
And pay your honey-tax to the hummingbird . . .

O now I see by the opening of blossoms,
And of bills of the hungry fledglings,
And the bright travel of sun-drunk insects,
Morning's business is afoot: Earth is busied with a
      million mouths!

Where goes eaten grass and thrush-snapped dragon-
      fly?
Creation eats itself, to spawn in swarming sun-rays . . .
Bull and cricket go to it: life lives on life . . .
But O, ye flame-daubed irises, and ye hosts of gnats,
Like a well of light moving in morning's light,
What is this garmented animal that comes eating and
      drinking among you?
What is this upright one, with spade and with shears?

He is the visible and the invisible,
Behind his mouth and his eyes are other mouth and
      eyes . . .
Thirster after visions
He sees the flowers to their roots and the Earth back
      through its silent ages:
He parts the sky with his gaze:

He flings a magic on the hills, clothing them with
 Upanishad music,
Peopling the valley with dreamed images that van-
 ished in Greece millenniums back;
And in the actual morning, out of longing, shapes on
 the hills
To-morrow's golden grandeur . . .

O ye million hungerers and ye sun-rays
Ye are the many mothers of this invisible god,
This Earth's star and sun that rises singing and toiling
 among you,
This that is I, in joy, in the garden,
Singing to you, ye morning-glories,
Calling to you, ye swinging spears of the larkspur.

James Oppenheim

PATTERNS [1]

I WALK down the garden paths,
And all the daffodils
Are blowing, and the bright blue squills.
I walk down the patterned garden-paths
In my stiff, brocaded gown.
With my powdered hair and jewelled fan,
I too am a rare
Pattern. As I wander down
The garden paths.

My dress is richly figured,
And the train

Makes a pink and silver stain
On the gravel, and the thrift
Of the borders.
Just a plate of current fashion,
Tripping by in high-heeled, ribboned shoes.
Not a softness anywhere about me,
Only whalebone and brocade.
And I sink on a seat in the shade
Of a lime tree. For my passion
Wars against the stiff brocade.
The daffodils and squills
Flutter in the breeze
As they please.
And I weep;
For the lime tree is in blossom
And one small flower has dropped upon my bosom.

And the plashing of waterdrops
In the marble fountain
Comes down the garden-paths.
The dripping never stops.
Underneath my stiffened gown
Is the softness of a woman bathing in a marble basin,
A basin in the midst of hedges grown
So thick, she cannot see her lover hiding,
But she guesses he is near,
And the sliding of the water
Seems the stroking of a dear
Hand upon her.
What is Summer in a fine brocaded gown!
I should like to see it lying in a heap upon the
        ground.
All the pink and silver crumpled up on the ground.

I would be the pink and silver as I ran along the
     paths,
And he would stumble after,
Bewildered by my laughter.
I should see the sun flashing from his sword-hilt and
     the buckles on his shoes.
I would choose
To lead him in a maze along the patterned paths,
A bright and laughing maze for my heavy-booted lover.
Till he caught me in the shade,
And the buttons of his waistcoat bruised my body as
     he clasped me,
Aching, melting, unafraid.
With the shadows of the leaves and the sundrops,
And the plopping of the waterdrops,
All about us in the open afternoon —
I am very like to swoon
With the weight of this brocade,
For the sun sifts through the shade.

Underneath the fallen blossom
In my bosom,
Is a letter I have hid.
It was brought to me this morning by a rider from
     the Duke.
"Madam, we regret to inform you that Lord Hartwell
Died in action Thursday se'nnight."
As I read it in the white, morning sunlight,
The letters squirmed like snakes.
"Any answer, Madam," said my footman.
"No," I told him.
"See that the messenger takes some refreshment.
No, no answer."

And I walked into the garden,
Up and down the patterned paths,
In my stiff, correct brocade.
The blue and yellow flowers stood up proudly in the
    sun,
Each one.
I stood upright too,
Held rigid to the pattern
By the stiffness of my gown.
Up and down I walked,
Up and down.

In a month he would have been my husband.
In a month, here, underneath this lime,
We would have broke the pattern;
He for me, and I for him,
He as Colonel, I as Lady,
On this shady seat.
He had a whim
That sunlight carried blessing.
And I answered, "It shall be as you have said."
Now he is dead.

In Summer and in Winter I shall walk
Up and down
The patterned garden-paths
In my stiff, brocaded gown.
The squills and daffodils
Will give place to pillared roses, and to asters, and
    to snow.
I shall go
Up and down
In my gown.

Gorgeously arrayed,
Boned and stayed.
And the softness of my body will be guarded from
     embrace
By each button, hook, and lace.
For the man who should loose me is dead,
Fighting with the Duke in Flanders,
In a pattern called a war.
Christ! What are patterns for?

                         Amy Lowell

RICHARD CORY

WHENEVER Richard Cory went down town,
We people on the pavement looked at him:
He was a gentleman from sole to crown,
Clean favored, and imperially slim.

And he was always quietly arrayed,
And he was always human when he talked;
But still he fluttered pulses when he said,
"Good-morning," and he glittered when he walked.

And he was rich, — yes, richer than a king, —
And admirably schooled in every grace:
In fine, we thought that he was everything
To make us wish that we were in his place.

So on we worked, and waited for the light,
And went without the meat, and cursed the bread;
And Richard Cory, one calm summer night,
Went home and put a bullet through his head.

                  Edwin Arlington Robinson

OF ONE SELF-SLAIN

WHEN he went blundering back to God,
　His songs half written, his work half done,
Who knows what paths his bruised feet trod,
　What hills of peace or pain he won?

I hope God smiled and took his hand,
　And said, "Poor truant, passionate fool!
Life's book is hard to understand:
　Why couldst thou not remain at school?"
　　　　　　　　　　Charles Hanson Towne

THE SILENT FOLK

OH, praise me not the silent folk;
　To me they only seem
Like leafless, bird-abandoned oak
　And muffled, frozen stream.

I want the leaves to talk and tell
　The joy that's in the tree,
And water-nymphs to weave a spell
　Of pixie melody.

Your silent folk may be sincere,
　But still, when all is said,
We have to grant they're rather drear, —
　And maybe, too, they're dead.
　　　　　　　　　　Charles Wharton Stork

CONVENTION

THE snow is lying very deep.
My house is sheltered from the blast.
I hear each muffled step outside,
I hear each voice go past.

But I'll not venture in the drift
Out of this bright security,
Till enough footsteps come and go
To make a path for me.

Agnes Lee

MAD BLAKE

BLAKE saw a treeful of angels at Peckham Rye,
And his hands could lay hold on the tiger's terrible
    heart.
Blake knew how deep is Hell, and Heaven how high,
And could build the universe from one tiny part.
Blake heard the asides of God, as with furrowed brow
He sifts the star-streams between the Then and the
    Now,
In vast infant sagacity brooding, an infant's grace
Shining serene on his simple, benignant face.

Blake was mad, they say, — and Space's Pandora-box
Loosed its wonders upon him — devils, but angels
    indeed.
I, they say, am sane, but no key of mine unlocks
One lock of one gate wherethrough Heaven's glory is
    freed.

And I stand and I hold my breath, daylong, yearlong,
Out of comfort and easy dreaming evermore starting
    awake, —
Yearning beyond all sanity for some echo of that Song
Of Songs that was sung to the soul of the madman,
    Blake!

Wm. Rose Benét

THE NAME

WHEN I come back from secret dreams
    In gardens deep and fair,
How very curious it seems —
    This mortal name I bear.

For by this name I make their bread
    And trim the household light
And sun the linen for the bed
    And close the door at night.

I wonder who myself may be,
    And whence it was I came —
Before the Church had laid on me
    This frail and earthly name.

My sponsors spake unto the Lord
    And three things promised they,
Upon my soul with one accord
    Their easy vows did lay.

My ancient spirit heard them not.
    I think it was not there.
But in a place they had forgot
    It drank a starrier air.

Yes, in a silent place and deep —
  There did it dance and run,
And sometimes it lay down to sleep
  Or sprang into the sun.

The Priest saw not my aureole shine!
  My sweet wings saw not he!
He graved me with a solemn sign
  And laid a name on me.

Now by this name I stitch and mend,
  The daughter of my home,
By this name do I save and spend
  And when they call, I come.

But oh, that Name, that other Name,
  More secret and more mine!
It burns as does the angelic flame
  Before the midmost shrine.

Before my soul to earth was brought
  Into God's heart it came,
He wrote a meaning in my thought
  And gave to me a Name.

By this Name do I ride the air
  And dance from star to star,
And I behold all things are fair,
  For I see them as they are.

I plunge into the deepest seas,
  In flames I, laughing, burn.
In roseate clouds I take my ease
  Nor to the earth return.

It is my beauteous Name — my own —
  That I have never heard.
God keeps it for Himself alone,
  That strange and lovely word.

God keeps it for Himself — but yet
  You are His voice, and so
In your heart He is calling me,
  And unto you I go.

Love, by this Name I sing, and breathe
  A fresh, mysterious air.
By this I innocently wreathe
  New garlands for my hair.

By this Name I am born anew
  More beautiful, more bright.
More roseate than angelic dew,
  Apparelled in delight.

I'll sing and stitch and make the **bread**
  In the wonder of my Name,
And sun the linen for the bed
  And tend the fireside flame.

By this Name do I answer yes —
  Word beautiful and true.
By this I'll sew the bridal dress
  I shall put on for you.
                    Anna Hempstead Branch

SONGS OF AN EMPTY HOUSE

VISTA

Before I die I may be great,
  The chanting guest of kings,
A queen in wonderlands of song
  Where every blossom sings.
I may put on a golden gown
  And walk in sunny light,
Carrying in my hair the day,
  And in my eyes the night.

It may be men will honor me —
  The wistful ones and wise,
Who know the ruth of victory,
  The joy of sacrifice.
I may be rich, I may be gay,
  But all the crowns grow old —
The laurel withers and the bay
  And dully rusts the gold.

Before I die I may break bread
  With many queens and kings —
Oh, take the golden gown away,
  For there are other things —
And I shall miss the love of babes
  With flesh of rose and pearl,
The dewy eyes, the budded lips —
  A boy, a little girl.

THE END

My father got me strong and straight and slim,
  And I give thanks to him:

My mother bore me glad and sound and sweet, —
    I kiss her feet.

But now, with me, their generation fails,
    And nevermore avails
To cast through me the ancient mould again,
    Such women and men.

I have no son, whose life of flesh and fire
    Sprang from my splendid sire,
No daughter for whose soul my mother's flesh
    Wrought raiment fresh.

Life's venerable rhythms like a flood
    Beat in my brain and blood,
Crying from all the generations past,
    "Is this the last?"

And I make answer to my haughty dead,
    Who made me, heart and head,
"Even the sunbeams falter, flicker and bend —
    I am the end."

                 Marguerite Wilkinson

THE HILL WIFE

LONELINESS

(*Her Word*)

ONE ought not to have to care
    So much as you and I
Care when the birds come round the house
    To seem to say good-bye;

Or care so much when they come back
  With whatever it is they sing;
The truth being we are as much
  Too glad for the one thing

As we are too sad for the other here —
  With birds that fill their breasts
But with each other and themselves
  And their built or driven nests.

HOUSE FEAR

ALWAYS — I tell you this they learned —
Always at night when they returned
To the lonely house from far away,
To lamps unlighted and fire gone gray,
They learned to rattle the lock and key
To give whatever might chance to be
Warning and time to be off in flight:
And preferring the out- to the in-door night,
They learned to leave the house-door wide
Until they had lit the lamp inside.

THE OFT-REPEATED DREAM

She had no saying dark enough
  For the dark pine that kept
Forever trying the window-latch
  Of the room where they slept.

The tireless but ineffectual hands
  That with every futile pass
Made the great tree seem as a little bird
  Before the mystery of glass!

It never had been inside the room,
  And only one of the two
Was afraid in an oft-repeated dream
  Of what the tree might do.

THE IMPULSE

It was too lonely for her there,
  And too wild,
And since there were but two of them,
  And no child,

And work was little in the house,
  She was free,
And followed where he furrowed field,
  Or felled tree.

She rested on a log and tossed
  The fresh chips,
With a song only to herself
  On her lips.

And once she went to break a bough
  Of black alder.
She strayed so far she scarcely heard
  When he called her —

And did n't answer — did n't speak —
  Or return.
She stood, and then she ran and hid
  In the fern.

He never found her, though he looked
  Everywhere,

And he asked at her mother's house
  Was she there.

Sudden and swift and light as that
  The ties gave,
And he learned of finalities
  Besides the grave.

Robert Frost

A LOVE SONG

MY love it should be silent, being deep —
And being very peaceful should be still —
Still as the utmost depths of ocean keep —
Serenely silent as some mighty hill.

Yet is my love so great it needs must fill
With very joy the inmost heart of me,
The joy of dancing branches on the hill
The joy of leaping waves upon the sea.

Theodosia Garrison

ENVOI

BELOVÈD, till the day break,
  Leave wide the little door;
And bless, to lack and longing,
  Our brimming more-and-more.

Is love a scanted portion,
  That we should hoard thereof? —
Oh, call unto the deserts,
  Belovèd and my Love!

Josephine Preston Peabody

OUR LITTLE HOUSE

Our little house upon the hill
In winter time is strangely still;
The roof tree, bare of leaves, stands high,
A candelabrum for the sky,
And down below the lamplights glow,
And ours makes answer o'er the snow.

Our little house upon the hill
In summer time strange voices fill;
With ceaseless rustle of the leaves,
And birds that twitter in the eaves,
And all the vines entangled so
The village lights no longer show.

Our little house upon the hill
Is just the house of Jack and Jill,
And whether showing or unseen,
Hid behind its leafy screen;
There's a star that points it out
When the lamp lights are in doubt.

Thomas Walsh

THE HOMELAND

My land was the west land; my home was on the hill.
I never think of my land but it makes my heart to
    thrill;
I never smell the west wind that blows the golden
    skies,
But old desire is in my feet and dreams are in my
    eyes.

My home crowned the high land; it had a stately
grace.
I never·think of my land but I see my mother's face;
I never smell the west wind that blows the silver ships
But old delight is in my heart and mirth is on my lips.

My land was a high land; my home was near the skies.
I never think of my land but a light is in my eyes;
I never smell the west wind that blows the summer
rain —
But I am at my mother's knee, a little lad again.

Dana Burnet

CRADLE SONG

I

LORD GABRIEL, wilt thou not rejoice
When at last a little boy's
    Cheek lies heavy as a rose
    And his eyelids close?

Gabriel, when that hush may be,
This sweet hand all heedfully
    I'll undo for thee alone,
    From his mother's own.

Then the far blue highway paven
With the burning stars of heaven,
    He shall gladden with the sweet
    Hasting of his feet: —

Feet so brightly bare and cool,
Leaping, as from pool to pool;

From a little laughing boy
    Splashing rainbow joy!

Gabriel, wilt thou understand
How to keep this hovering hand? —
    Never shut, as in a bond,
      From the bright beyond? —

Nay, but though it cling and close
Tightly as a climbing rose,
    Clasp it only so, — aright,
      Lest his heart take fright.

    (*Dormi, dormi, tu.*
    The dusk is hung with blue.)

II

Lord Michael, wilt not thou rejoice
When at last a little boy's
    Heart, a shut-in murmuring bee,
      Turns him unto thee?

Wilt thou heed thine armor well, —
To take his hand from Gabriel,
    So his radiant cup of dream
      May not spill a gleam?

He will take thy heart in thrall,
Telling o'er thy breastplate, all
    Colors, in his bubbling speech,
      With his hand to each.

    (*Dormi, dormi, tu.*
    Sapphire is the blue,

Pearl and beryl, they are called,
Crysoprase and emerald,
Sard and amethyst
  Numbered so, and kissed.)

Ah, but find some angel-word
For thy sharp, subduing sword!
  Yea, Lord Michael, make no doubt
  He will find it out:

  (*Dormi, dormi, tu!*
  His eyes will look at you.)

III

Last, a little morning space,
Lead him to that leafy place
  Where Our Lady sits awake,
  For all mothers' sake.

Bosomed with the Blessèd One,
He shall mind her of her Son,
  Once so folded from all harms
  In her shrining arms.

  (*In her veil of blue,*
  Dormi, dormi, tu.)

  So; — and fare thee well.
  Softly, — Gabriel . . .
When the first faint red shall come,
Bid the Day-star lead him home,
  For the bright world's sake,
  To my heart, awake.
    Josephine Preston Peabody

SLUMBER SONG

DROWSILY come the sheep
From the place where the pastures be,
    By a dusty lane
    To the fold again,
First one, and then two, and three:
    First one, then two, by the paths of sleep
    Drowsily come the sheep.

Drowsily come the sheep,
And the shepherd is singing low:
    After eight comes nine
    In the endless line,
They come, and then in they go.
    First eight, then nine, by the paths of sleep
    Drowsily come the sheep.

Drowsily come the sheep
And they pass through the sheepfold door;
    After one comes two,
    After one comes two,
Comes two and then three and four.
    First one, then two, by the paths of sleep,
    Drowsily come the sheep.

Louis V. Ledoux

BALLAD OF A CHILD [1]

YEARLY thrilled the plum tree
With the mother-mood;
Every June the rose stock

[1] Reprinted, by permission of the publishers, from *The Quest*, by John G. Neihardt. Copyright, 1916, by The Macmillan Company.

Bore her wonder-child:
Every year the wheatlands
Reared a golden brood:
World of praying Rachaels,
Heard and reconciled!

"Poet," said the plum tree's
Singing white and green,
"What avails your mooning,
Can you fashion plums?"
"Dreamer," crooned the wheatland's
Rippling vocal sheen,
"See my golden children
Marching as with drums!"

"By a god begotten,"
Hymned the sunning vine,
"In my lyric children
Purple music flows!"
"Singer," breathed the rose bush,
"Are they not divine?"
"Have you any daughters
Mighty as a rose?"

Happy, happy mothers!
Cruel, cruel words!
Mine are ghostly children,
Haunting all the ways;
Latent in the plum bloom,
Calling through the birds,
Romping with the wheat brood
In their shadow plays!

Gotten out of star-glint,
Mothered of the Moon;
Nurtured with the rose scent,
Wild elusive throng!
Something of the vine's dream
Crept into a tune;
Something of the wheat-drone
Echoed in a song.

Once again the white fires
Smoked among the plums;
Once again the world-joy
Burst the crimson bud;
Golden-bannered wheat broods
Marched to fairy drums;
Once again the vineyard
Felt the Bacchic blood.

"Lo, he comes, — the dreamer" —
Crooned the whitened boughs,
"Quick with vernal love-fires —
Oh, at last he knows!
See the bursting plum bloom
There above his brows!"
"Boaster!" breathed the rose bush,
"'Tis a budding rose!"

Droned the glinting acres,
"In his soul, mayhap,
Something like a wheat-dream
Quickens into shape!"
Sang the sunning vineyard,
"Lo, the lyric sap

Sets his heart a-throbbing
Like a purple grape!"

Mother of the wheatlands,
Mother of the plums,
Mother of the vineyard —
All that loves and grows —
Such a living glory
To the dreamer comes,
Mystic as a wheat-song,
Mighty as a rose!

Star-glint, moon-glow,
Gathered in a mesh!
Spring-hope, white fire
By a kiss beguiled!
Something of the world-joy
Dreaming into flesh!
Bird-song, vine-thrill
Quickened to a child!

John G. Neihardt

AMBITION

KENTON and Deborah, Michael and Rose,
These are fine children as all the world knows,
But into my arms in my dreams every night
Come Peter and Christopher, Faith and Delight.

Kenton is tropical, Rose is pure white,
Deborah shines like a star in the night;
Michael's round eyes are as blue as the sea,
And nothing on earth could be dearer to me.

But where is the baby with Faith can compare?
What is the colour of Peterkin's hair?
Who can make Christopher clear to my sight,
Or show me the eyes of my daughter Delight?

When people inquire I always just state:
"I have four nice children and hope to have eight.
Though the first four are pretty and certain to please,
Who knows but the rest may be nicer than these?"

Aline Kilmer

THE GIFT

LET others give you wealth and love,
    And guard you while you live;
I cannot set my gift above
    The gifts that others give.

And yet the gift I give is good:
    In one man's eyes to see
The worship of your maidenhood
    While children climb your knee.

Louis V. Ledoux

THE ANCIENT BEAUTIFUL THINGS

I AM all alone in the room.
The evening stretches before me
Like a road all delicate gloom
Till it reaches the midnight's gate.
And I hear his step on the path,
And his questioning whistle, low
At the door as I hurry to meet him.

He will ask, "Are the doors all locked?
Is the fire made safe on the hearth?
And she — is she sound asleep?"

I shall say, "Yes, the doors are locked,
And the ashes are white as the frost:
Only a few red eyes
To stare at the empty room.
And she is all sound asleep,
Up there where the silence sings,
And the curtains stir in the cold."

He will ask, "And what did you do
While I have been gone so long?
So long! Four hours or five!"

I shall say, "There was nothing I did. —
I mended that sleeve of your coat.
And I made her a little white hood
Of the furry pieces I found
Up in the garret to-day.
She shall wear it to play in the snow,
Like a little white bear, — and shall laugh,
And tumble, and crystals of stars
Shall shine on her cheeks and hair.
— It was nothing I did. — I thought
You would never come home again!"

Then he will laugh out, low,
Being fond of my folly, perhaps;
And softly and hand in hand
We shall creep upstairs in the dusk
To look at her, lying asleep:
Our little gold bird in her nest:

The wonderful bird who flew in
At the window our Life flung wide.
(How should we have chosen her,
Had we seen them all in a row,
The unborn vague little souls,
All wings and tremulous hands?
How should we have chosen her,
Made like a star to shine,
Made like a bird to fly,
Out of a drop of our blood,
And earth, and fire, and God?)

Then we shall go to sleep,
Glad. —
   O God, did you know
When you moulded men out of clay,
Urging them up and up
Through the endless circles of change,
Travail and turmoil and death,
Many would curse you down,
Many would live all gray
With their faces flat like a mask:
But there would be some, O God,
Crying to you each night,
"I am so glad! so glad!
I am so rich and gay!
How shall I thank you, God?"

Was that one thing you knew
When you smiled and found it was good:
The curious teeming earth
That grew like a child at your hand?
Ah, you might smile, for that! —

— I am all alone in the room.
The books and the pictures peer,
Dumb old friends, from the dark.
The wind goes high on the hills,
And my fire leaps out, being proud.
The terrier, down on the hearth,
Twitches and barks in his sleep,
Soft little foolish barks,
More like a dream than a dog . . .

I will mend the sleeve of that coat,
All ragged, — and make her the hood
Furry, and white, for the snow.
She shall tumble and laugh . . .
                                    Oh, I think
Though a thousand rivers of grief
Flood over my head, — though a hill
Of horror lie on my breast, —
Something will sing, "Be glad!
You have had all your heart's desire:
The unknown things that you asked
When you lay awake in the nights,
Alone, and searching the dark
For the secret wonder of life.
You have had them (can you forget?):
The ancient beautiful things!" . . .

How long he is gone. And yet
It is only an hour or two. . . .

Oh, I am so happy. My eyes
Are troubled with tears.
                        Did you know,

O God, they would be like this,
Your ancient beautiful things?
Are there more? Are there more, — out there? —
O God, are there always more?
                              Fannie Stearns Davis

MATER DOLOROSA [1]

O CLINGING hands, and eyes where sleep has set
    Her seal of peace, go not from me so soon.
O little feet, take not the pathway yet,
The dust of other feet with tears is wet,
And sorrow wanders there with slow regret;
    O eager feet, take not the path so soon.

Take it not yet, for death is at the end,
    And kingly death will wait until you come.
Full soon the feet of youth will turn the bend,
The eyes will see where followed footsteps wend.
Go not so soon, though death be found a friend;
    For kingly death will wait until you come.
                              Louis V. Ledoux

PREVISION

I KNOW you are too dear to stay;
    You are so exquisitely sweet:
My lonely house will thrill some day
    To echoes of your eager feet.

I hold your words within my heart,
    So few, so infinitely dear;
Watching your fluttering hands I start
    At the corroding touch of fear.

[1] Reprinted, by permission of the publishers, from *The Story of Eleusis,* by Louis V. Ledoux. Copyright, 1916, by The Macmillan Company.

A faint, unearthly music rings
   From you to Heaven — it is not far!
A mist about your beauty clings
   Like a thin cloud before a star.

My heart shall keep the child I knew,
   When you are really gone from me,
And spend its life remembering you
   As shells remember the lost sea.

                         Aline Kilmer

"A WIND ROSE IN THE NIGHT"

A WIND rose in the night,
   (She had always feared it so!)
Sorrow plucked at my heart
   And I could not help but go.

Softly I went and stood
   By her door at the end of the hall.
Dazed with grief I watched
   The candles flaring and tall.

The wind was wailing aloud:
   I thought how she would have cried
For my warm familiar arms
   And the sense of me by her side.

The candles flickered and leapt,
   The shadows jumped on the wall.
She lay before me small and still
   And did not care at all.

                         Aline Kilmer

HOW MUCH OF GODHOOD

How much of Godhood did it take —
    What purging epochs had to pass,
Ere I was fit for leaf and lake
    And worthy of the patient grass?

What mighty travails must have been,
    What ages must have moulded me,
Ere I was raised and made akin
    To dawn, the daisy and the sea.

In what great struggles was I felled,
    In what old lives I labored long,
Ere I was given a world that held
    A meadow, butterflies and Song?

But oh, what cleansings and what fears,
    What countless raisings from the dead,
Ere I could see Her, touched with tears,
    Pillow the little weary head.

                              Louis Untermeyer

THE FIRST FOOD

MOTHER, in some sad evening long ago,
    From thy young breast my groping lips were taken,
    Their hunger stilled, so soon again to waken,
But nevermore that holy food to know.

Ah! nevermore! for all the child might crave!
    Ah! nevermore! through years unkind and dreary!
    Often of other fare my lips are weary,
Unwearied once of what thy bosom gave.

(Poor wordless mouth that could not speak thy name!
  At what unhappy revels has it eaten
  The viands that no memory can sweeten, —
The banquet found eternally the same!)

Then fell a shadow first on thee and me,
  And tendrils broke that held us two how dearly!
  Once infinitely thine, then hourly, yearly,
Less thine, as less the worthy thine to be.

(O mouth that yet should kiss the mouth of Sin!
  Were lies so sweet, now bitter to remember?
  Slow sinks the flame unfaithful to an ember;
New beauty fades and passion's wine is thin.)

How poor an end of that solicitude
  And all the love I had not from another!
  Peace to thine unforgetting heart, O Mother,
Who gav'st the dear and unremembered food!

George Sterling

THE MONK IN THE KITCHEN

I

ORDER is a lovely thing;
On disarray it lays its wing,
Teaching simplicity to sing.
It has a meek and lowly grace,
Quiet as a nun's face.
Lo — I will have thee in this place!
Tranquil well of deep delight,
Transparent as the water, bright —

All things that shine through thee appear
As stones through water, sweetly clear.
Thou clarity,
That with angelic charity
Revealest beauty where thou art,
Spread thyself like a clean pool.
Then all the things that in thee are
Shall seem more spiritual and fair,
Reflections from serener air —
Sunken shapes of many a star
In the high heavens set afar.

II

Ye stolid, homely, visible things,
Above you all brood glorious wings
Of your deep entities, set high,
Like slow moons in a hidden sky.
But you, their likenesses, are spent
Upon another element.
Truly ye are but seemings —
The shadowy cast-off gleamings
Of bright solidities. Ye seem
Soft as water, vague as dream;
Image, cast in a shifting stream.

III

What are ye?
I know not.
Brazen pan and iron pot,
Yellow brick and grey flag-stone
That my feet have trod upon —
Ye seem to me
Vessels of bright mystery.

For ye do bear a shape, and so
Though ye were made by man, I know
An inner Spirit also made
And ye his breathings have obeyed.

IV

Shape the strong and awful Spirit,
Laid his ancient hand on you.
He waste chaos doth inherit;
He can alter and subdue.
Verily, he doth lift up
Matter, like a sacred cup.
Into deep substance he reached, and lo
Where ye were not, ye were; and so
Out of useless nothing, ye
Groaned and laughed and came to be.
And I use you, as I can,
Wonderful uses, made for man,
Iron pot and brazen pan.

V

What are ye?
I know not;
Nor what I really do
When I move and govern you.
There is no small work unto God.
He requires of us greatness;
Of his least creature
A high angelic nature,
Stature superb and bright completeness.
He sets to us no humble duty.
Each act that he would have us do
Is haloed round with strangest beauty.

Terrific deeds and cosmic tasks
Of his plainest child he asks.
When I polish the brazen pan
I hear a creature laugh afar
In the gardens of a star,
And from his burning presence run
Flaming wheels of many a sun.
Whoever makes a thing more bright,
He is an angel of all light.
When I cleanse this earthen floor
My spirit leaps to see
Bright garments trailing over it.
Wonderful lustres cover it,
A cleanness made by me.
Purger of all men's thoughts and ways,
With labor do I sound Thy praise,
My work is done for Thee.
Whoever makes a thing more bright,
He is an angel of all light.
Therefore let me spread abroad
The beautiful cleanness of my God.

VI

One time in the cool of dawn
Angels came and worked with me.
The air was soft with many a wing.
They laughed amid my solitude
And cast bright looks on everything.
Sweetly of me did they ask
That they might do my common task.
And all were beautiful — but one
With garments whiter than the sun

Had such a face
Of deep, remembered grace,
That when I saw I cried — "Thou art
The great Blood-Brother of my heart.
Where have I seen thee?" — And he said,
"When we are dancing 'round God's throne,
How often thou art there.
Beauties from thy hands have flown
Like white doves wheeling in mid-air.
Nay — thy soul remembers not?
Work on, and cleanse thy iron pot."

VII

What are we? I know not.

Anna Hempstead Branch

A SAINT'S HOURS

IN the still cold before the sun
Her Matins   Her brothers and her sisters small
She woke, and washed and dressed each
one.

And through the morning hours all
Prime   Singing above her broom she stood
And swept the house from hall to hall.

Then out she ran with tidings good
Tierce   Across the field and down the lane,
To share them with the neighborhood.

Four miles she walked, and home again,
Sexts   To sit through half the afternoon
And hear a feeble crone complain.

Nones
> But when she saw the frosty moon
>   And lakes of shadow on the hill,
> Her maiden dreams grew bright as noon.

Vespers
> She threw her pitying apron frill
>   Over a little trembling mouse
> When the sleek cat yawned on the sill.

Evensong
> In the late hours and drowsy house,
>   At last, too tired, beside her bed
> She fell asleep — her prayers half said.
>   *Sarah N. Cleghorn*

A LADY [1]

You are beautiful and faded
Like an old opera tune
Played upon a harpsichord;
Or like the sun-flooded silks
Of an eighteenth-century boudoir.
In your eyes
Smoulder the fallen roses of out-lived minutes,
And the perfume of your soul
Is vague and suffusing,
With the pungence of sealed spice-jars.
Your half-tones delight me,
And I grow mad with gazing
At your blent colours.

[1] Reprinted, by permission of the publishers, from *Sword Blades and Poppy Seed*, by Amy Lowell. Copyright, 1914, by The Macmillan Company.

My vigour is a new-minted penny,
Which I cast at your feet.
Gather it up from the dust,
That its sparkle may amuse you.

Amy Lowell

THE CHILD IN ME

SHE follows me about my House of Life
(This happy little ghost of my dead Youth!)
She has no part in Time's relentless strife
She keeps her old simplicity and truth —
And laughs at grim Mortality,
This deathless Child that stays with me —
(This happy little ghost of my dead Youth!)

My House of Life is weather-stained with years —
(O Child in Me, I wonder why you stay.)
Its windows are bedimmed with rain of tears,
The walls have lost their rose, its thatch is gray.
One after one its guests depart,
So dull a host is my old heart.
(O Child in Me, I wonder why you stay!)

For jealous Age, whose face I would forget,
Pulls the bright flowers you bring me from my hair
And powders it with snow; and yet — and yet
I love your dancing feet and jocund air.
I have no taste for caps of lace
To tie about my faded face —
I love to wear your flowers in my hair.

O Child in Me, leave not my House of Clay
Until we pass together through the Door,
When lights are out, and Life has gone away
And we depart to come again no more.
We comrades who have travelled far
Will hail the Twilight and the Star,
And smiling, pass together through the Door!

May Riley Smith

THE SON

I HEARD an old farm-wife,
   Selling some barley,
Mingle her life with life
   And the name "Charley."

Saying, "The crop's all in,
   We're about through now;
Long nights will soon begin,
   We're just us two now.

Twelve bushels at sixty cents,
   It's all I carried —
He sickened making fence;
   He was to be married —

It feels like frost was near —
   His hair was curly.
The spring was late that year,
   But the harvest early."

Ridgely Torrence

MUY VIEJA MEXICANA

I'VE seen her pass with eyes upon the road —
An old bent woman in a bronze-black shawl,
With skin as dried and wrinkled as a mummy's,
As brown as a cigar-box, and her voice
Like the low vibrant strings of a guitar.
And I have fancied from the girls about
What she was at their age, what they will be
When they are old as she. But now she sits
And smokes away each night till dawn comes round,
Thinking, beside the piñons' flame, of days
Long past and gone, when she was young — content
To be no longer young, her epic done:

For a woman has work and much to do,
And it's good at the last to know it's through,
And still have time to sit alone,
To have some time you can call your own.
It's good at the last to know your mind
And travel the paths that you traveled blind,
To see each turn and even make
Trips in the byways you did not take —
But that, *por Dios*, is over and done,
It's pleasanter now in the way we've come;
It's good to smoke and none to say
What's to be done on the coming day,
No mouths to feed or coat to mend,
And none to call till the last long end.
Though one have sons and friends of one's own,
It's better at last to live alone.
For a man must think of food to buy,
And a woman's thoughts may be wild and high;

But when she is young she must curb her pride,
And her heart is tamed for the child at her side.
But when she is old her thoughts may go
Wherever they will, and none to know.
And night is the time to think and dream,
And not to get up with the dawn's first gleam;
Night is the time to laugh or weep,
And when dawn comes it is time to sleep . . .

When it's all over and there's none to care,
I mean to be like her and take my share
Of comfort when the long day's done,
And smoke away the nights, and see the sun
Far off, a shrivelled orange in a sky gone black,
Through eyes that open inward and look back.

Alice Corbin

HROLF'S THRALL, HIS SONG

THERE be five things to a man's desire:
Kine flesh, roof-tree, his own fire,
Clean cup of sweet wine from goat's hide,
And through dark night one to lie beside.

Four things poor and homely be:
Hearth-fire, white cheese, own roof-tree,
True mead slow brewed with brown malt;
But a good woman is savour and salt.

Plow, shove deep through gray loam;
Hack, sword, hack for straw-thatch home;
Guard, buckler, guard both beast and human —
God, send true man his true woman!

Willard Wattles

THE INTERPRETER

In the very early morning when the light was low
She got all together and she went like snow,
Like snow in the springtime on a sunny hill,
And we were only frightened and can't think still.

We can't think quite that the katydids and frogs
And the little crying chickens and the little grunting
       hogs,
And the other living things that she spoke for to us
Have nothing more to tell her since it happened thus.

She never is around for any one to touch,
But of ecstasy and longing she too knew much,
And always when any one has time to call his own
She will come and be beside him as quiet as a stone.

Orrick Johns

OLD KING COLE [1]

In Tilbury Town did Old King Cole
    A wise old age anticipate,
Desiring, with his pipe and bowl,
    No Khan's extravagant estate.
No crown annoyed his honest head,
    No fiddlers three were called or needed;
For two disastrous heirs instead
    Made music more than ever three did.

[1] Reprinted, by permission of the publishers, from *The Man Against the Sky*, by Edwin Arlington Robinson. Copyright, 1916, by The Macmillan Company.

Bereft of her with whom his life
Was harmony without a flaw,
He took no other for a wife,
Nor sighed for any that he saw;
And if he doubted his two sons,
And heirs, Alexis and Evander,
He might have been as doubtful once
Of Robert Burns and Alexander.

Alexis, in his early youth,
Began to steal — from old and young.
Likewise Evander, and the truth
Was like a bad taste on his tongue.
Born thieves and liars, their affair
Seemed only to be tarred with evil —
The most insufferable pair
Of scamps that ever cheered the devil.

The world went on, their fame went on,
And they went on — from bad to worse;
Till, goaded hot with nothing done,
And each accoutred with a curse,
The friends of Old King Cole, by twos,
And fours, and sevens, and elevens,
Pronounced unalterable views
Of doings that were not of heaven's.

And having learned again whereby
Their baleful zeal had come about,
King Cole met many a wrathful eye
So kindly that its wrath went out —
Or partly out. Say what they would,
He seemed the more to court their candor;

But never told what kind of good
Was in Alexis and Evander.

And Old King Cole, with many a puff
That haloed his urbanity,
Would smoke till he had smoked enough,
And listen most attentively.
He beamed as with an inward light
That had the Lord's assurance in it;
And once a man was there all night,
Expecting something every minute.

But whether from too little thought,
Or too much fealty to the bowl,
A dim reward was all he got
For sitting up with Old King Cole.
"Though mine," the father mused aloud,
"Are not the sons I would have chosen,
Shall I, less evilly endowed,
By their infirmity be frozen?

"They'll have a bad end, I'll agree,
But I was never born to groan;
For I can see what I can see,
And I'm accordingly alone.
With open heart and open door,
I love my friends, I like my neighbors;
But if I try to tell you more,
Your doubts will overmatch my labors.

"This pipe would never make me calm,
This bowl my grief would never drown.
For grief like mine there is no balm
In Gilead, or in Tilbury Town.

And if I see what I can see,
I know not any way to blind it;
Nor more if any way may be
For you to grope or fly to find it.

"There may be room for ruin yet,
And ashes for a wasted love;
Or, like One whom you may forget,
I may have meat you know not of.
And if I'd rather live than weep
Meanwhile, do you find that surprising?
Why, bless my soul, the man's asleep!
That's good. The sun will soon be rising."

Edwin Arlington Robinson

SPOON RIVER ANTHOLOGY [1]

WASHINGTON McNEELY

RICH, honored by my fellow citizens,
The father of many children, born of a noble mother,
All raised there
In the great mansion-house, at the edge of town.
Note the cedar tree on the lawn!
I sent all the boys to Ann Arbor, all of the girls to
        Rockford,
The while my life went on, getting more riches and
        honors —
Resting under my cedar tree at evening.
The years went on.
I sent the girls to Europe;
I dowered them when married.

[1] Reprinted, by permission of the publishers, from *Spoon River Anthology*,
by Edgar Lee Masters. Copyright, 1915, by The Macmillan Company.

I gave the boys money to start in business.
They were strong children, promising as apples
Before the bitten places show.
But John fled the country in disgrace.
Jenny died in child-birth —
I sat under my cedar tree.
Harry killed himself after a debauch,
Susan was divorced —
I sat under my cedar tree.
Paul was invalided from over study,
Mary became a recluse at home for love of a man —
I sat under my cedar tree.
All were gone, or broken-winged or devoured by life —
I sat under my cedar tree.
My mate, the mother of them, was taken —
I sat under my cedar tree,
Till ninety years were tolled.
O maternal Earth, which rocks the fallen leaf to sleep!

HARMON WHITNEY

OUT of the lights and roar of cities,
Drifting down like a spark in Spoon River,
Burnt out with the fire of drink, and broken,
The paramour of a woman I took in self-contempt,
But to hide a wounded pride as well.
To be judged and loathed by a village of little minds —
I, gifted with tongues and wisdom,
Sunk here to the dust of the justice court,
A picker of rags in the rubbage of spites and wrongs, —
I, whom fortune smiled on! I in a village,
Spouting to gaping yokels pages of verse,
Out of the lore of golden years,
Or raising a laugh with a flash of filthy wit

When they brought the drinks to kindle my dying
    mind.
To be judged by you,
The soul of me hidden from you,
With its wound gangrened
By love for a wife who made the wound,
With her cold white bosom, treasonous, pure and hard,
Relentless to the last, when the touch of her hand
At any time, might have cured me of the typhus,
Caught in the jungle of life where many are lost.
And only to think that my soul could not react,
As Bryon's did, in song, in something noble,
But turned on itself like a tortured snake —
Judge me this way, O world!

THOMAS TREVELYAN

READING in Ovid the sorrowful story of Itys,
Son of the love of Tereus and Procne, slain
For the guilty passion of Tereus for Philomela,
The flesh of him served to Tereus by Procne,
And the wrath of Tereus, the murderess pursuing
Till the gods made Philomela a nightingale,
Lute of the rising moon, and Procne a swallow!
Oh livers and artists of Hellas centuries gone,
Sealing in little thuribles dreams and wisdom,
Incense beyond all price, forever fragrant,
A breath whereof makes clear the eyes of the soul!
How I inhaled its sweetness here in Spoon River!
The thurible opening when I had lived and learned
How all of us kill the children of love, and all of us,
Knowing not what we do, devour their flesh;
And all of us change to singers, although it be
But once in our lives, or change — alas — to swallows,
To twitter amid cold winds and falling leaves!

ALEXANDER THROCKMORTON

IN youth my wings were strong and tireless,
But I did not know the mountains.
In age I knew the mountains
But my weary wings could not follow my vision —
Genius is wisdom and youth.

RUTHERFORD McDOWELL

THEY brought me ambrotypes
Of the old pioneers to enlarge.
And sometimes one sat for me —
Some one who was in being
When giant hands from the womb of the world
Tore the republic.
What was it in their eyes? —
For I could never fathom
That mystical pathos of drooped eyelids,
And the serene sorrow of their eyes.
It was like a pool of water,
Amid oak trees at the edge of a forest,
Where the leaves fall,
As you hear the crow of a cock
Where the third generation lives, and the strong
          men
From a far-off farm-house, seen near the hills
And the strong women are gone and forgotten.
And these grand-children and great grand-children
Of the pioneers!
Truly did my camera record their faces, too,
With so much of the old strength gone,
And the old faith gone,
And the old mastery of life gone,
And the old courage gone,

Which labors and loves and suffers and sings
Under the sun!

WILLIAM H. HERNDON

THERE by the window in the old house
Perched on the bluff, overlooking miles of valley,
My days of labor closed, sitting out life's decline,
Day by day did I look in my memory,
As one who gazes in an enchantress' crystal globe,
And I saw the figures of the past,
As if in a pageant glassed by a shining dream,
Move through the incredible sphere of time.
And I saw a man arise from the soil like a fabled
        giant
And throw himself over a deathless destiny,
Master of great armies, head of the republic,
Bringing together into a dithyramb of recreative song
The epic hopes of a people;
At the same time Vulcan of sovereign fires,
Where imperishable shields and swords were beaten
        out
From spirits tempered in heaven.
Look in the crystal! See how he hastens on
To the place where his path comes up to the path
Of a child of Plutarch and Shakespeare.
O Lincoln, actor indeed, playing well your part,
And Booth, who strode in a mimic play within the
        play,
Often and often I saw you,
As the cawing crows winged their way to the wood
Over my house-top at solemn sunsets,
There by my window,
Alone.

ANNE RUTLEDGE

OUT of me unworthy and unknown
The vibrations of deathless music:
"With malice toward none, with charity for all."
Out of me the forgiveness of millions toward millions,
And the beneficent face of a nation
Shining with justice and truth.
I am Anne Rutledge who sleep beneath these weeds,
Beloved in life of Abraham Lincoln,
Wedded to him, not through union,
But through separation.
Bloom forever, O Republic,
From the dust of my bosom!

Edgar Lee Masters

LINCOLN

I

LIKE a gaunt, scraggly pine
Which lifts its head above the mournful sandhills;
And patiently, through dull years of bitter silence,
Untended and uncared for, starts to grow.

Ungainly, labouring, huge,
The wind of the north has twisted and gnarled its
        branches;
Yet in the heat of midsummer days, when thunder-
        clouds ring the horizon,
A nation of men shall rest beneath its shade.
And it shall protect them all,
Hold everyone safe there, watching aloof in silence;
Until at last one mad stray bolt from the zenith
Shall strike it in an instant down to earth.

II

There was a darkness in this man; an immense and
    hollow darkness,
Of which we may not speak, nor share with him, nor
    enter;
A darkness through which strong roots stretched down-
    wards into the earth
Towards old things:

Towards the herdman-kings who walked the earth
    and spoke with God,
Towards the wanderers who sought for they knew not
    what, and found their goal at last;
Towards the men who waited, only waited patiently
    when all seemed lost,
Many bitter winters of defeat;

Down to the granite of patience
These roots swept, knotted fibrous roots, prying,
    piercing, seeking,
And drew from the living rock and the living waters
    about it
The red sap to carry upwards to the sun.

Not proud, but humble,
Only to serve and pass on, to endure to the end
    through service;
For the ax is laid at the roots of the trees, and all that
    bring not forth good fruit
Shall be cut down on the day to come and cast into
    the fire.

III

There is a silence abroad in the land to-day,
And in the hearts of men, a deep and anxious silence;
And, because we are still at last, those bronze lips
     slowly open,
Those hollow and weary eyes take on a gleam of light.

Slowly a patient, firm-syllabled voice cuts through
     the endless silence
Like labouring oxen that drag a plow through the
     chaos of rude clay-fields:
"I went forward as the light goes forward in early
     spring,
But there were also many things which I left behind.

"Tombs that were quiet;
One, of a mother, whose brief light went out in the
     darkness,
One, of a loved one, the snow on whose grave is long
     falling,
One, only of a child, but it was mine.

"Have you forgot your graves? Go, question them in
     anguish,
Listen long to their unstirred lips. From your hostages
     to silence,
Learn there is no life without death, no dawn without
     sun-setting,
No victory but to him who has given all."

IV

The clamour of cannon dies down, the furnace-mouth
     of the battle is silent.

The midwinter sun dips and descends, the earth takes
on afresh its bright colours.

But he whom we mocked and obeyed not, he whom
we scorned and mistrusted,

He has descended, like a god, to his rest.

Over the uproar of cities,

Over the million intricate threads of life wavering and
crossing,

In the midst of problems we know not, tangling, per-
plexing, ensnaring,

Rises one white tomb alone.

Beam over it, stars,

Wrap it round, stripes — stripes red for the pain that
he bore for you —

Enfold it forever, O flag, rent, soiled, but repaired
through your anguish;

Long as you keep him there safe, the nations shall bow
to your law.

Strew over him flowers:

Blue forget-me-nots from the north, and the bright
pink arbutus

From the east, and from the west rich orange blossom,

And from the heart of the land take the passion-
flower;

Rayed, violet, dim,

With the nails that pierced, the cross that he bore and
the circlet,

And beside it there lay also one lonely snow-white
   magnolia,
Bitter for remembrance of the healing which has
   passed.

John Gould Fletcher

ABRAHAM LINCOLN WALKS AT
MIDNIGHT [1]

It is portentous, and a thing of state
That here at midnight, in our little town
A mourning figure walks, and will not rest,
Near the old court-house pacing up and down,

Or by his homestead, or in shadowed yards
He lingers where his children used to play,
Or through the market, on the well-worn stones
He stalks until the dawn-stars burn away.

A bronzed, lank man! His suit of ancient black,
A famous high-top hat and plain worn shawl
Make him the quaint great figure that men love,
The prairie lawyer, master of us all.

He cannot sleep upon his hillside now.
He is among us: — as in times before!
And we who toss and lie awake for long
Breathe deep, and start, to see him pass the door.

His head is bowed. He thinks on men and kings.
Yea, when the sick world cries, how can he sleep?

Too many peasants fight, they know not why,
Too many homesteads in black terror weep.

The sins of all the war-lords burn his heart.
He sees the dreadnaughts scouring every main.
He carries on his shawl-wrapped shoulders now
The bitterness, the folly and the pain.

He cannot rest until a spirit-dawn
Shall come; — the shining hope of Europe free:
The league of sober folk, the Workers' Earth,
Bringing long peace to Cornland, Alp and Sea.

It breaks his heart that kings must murder still,
That all his hours of travail here for men
Seem yet in vain. And who will bring white peace
That he may sleep upon his hill again?

Vachel Lindsay

PRAYER DURING BATTLE

Lord, in this hour of tumult,
    Lord, in this night of fears,
Keep open, oh, keep open
    My eyes, my ears.

Not blindly, not in hatred,
    Lord, let me do my part.
Keep open, oh, keep open
    My mind, my heart!

Hermann Hagedorn

PRAYER OF A SOLDIER IN FRANCE

My shoulders ache beneath my pack
(Lie easier, Cross, upon His back).

I march with feet that burn and smart
(Tread, Holy Feet, upon my heart).

Men shout at me who may not speak
(They scourged Thy back and smote Thy cheek).

I may not lift a hand to clear
My eyes of salty drops that sear.

(Then shall my fickle soul forget
Thy Agony of Bloody Sweat?)

My rifle hand is stiff and numb
(From Thy pierced palm red rivers come).

Lord, Thou didst suffer more for me
Than all the hosts of land and sea.

So let me render back again
This millionth of Thy gift. Amen.

Joyce Kilmer

THE WHITE COMRADE

Under our curtain of fire,
Over the clotted clods,
We charged, to be withered, to reel
And despairingly wheel
When the bugles bade us retire
From the terrible odds.

As we ebbed with the battle-tide,
Fingers of red-hot steel
Suddenly closed on my side.
I fell, and began to pray.
I crawled on my hands and lay
Where a shallow crater yawned wide;
Then I swooned. . . .

When I woke, it was yet day.
Fierce was the pain of my wound,
But I saw it was death to stir,
For fifty paces away
Their trenches were.
In torture I prayed for the dark
And the stealthy step of my friend
Who, stanch to the very end,
Would creep to the danger zone
And offer his life as a mark
To save my own.

Night fell. I heard his tread,
Not stealthy, but firm and serene,
As if my comrade's head
Were lifted far from that scene
Of passion and pain and dread;
As if my comrade's heart
In carnage took no part;
As if my comrade's feet
Were set on some radiant street
Such as no darkness might haunt;
As if my comrade's eyes,
No deluge of flame could surprise,
No death and destruction daunt,

No red-beaked bird dismay,
Nor sight of decay.

Then in the bursting shells' dim light
I saw he was clad in white.
For a moment I thought that I saw the smock
Of a shepherd in search of his flock.
Alert were the enemy, too,
And their bullets flew
Straight at a mark no bullet could fail;
For the seeker was tall and his robe was bright;
But he did not flee nor quail.
Instead, with unhurrying stride
He came,
And gathering my tall frame,
Like a child, in his arms . . .

I slept,
And awoke
From a blissful dream
In a cave by a stream.
My silent comrade had bound my side.
No pain now was mine, but a wish that I spoke, —
A mastering wish to serve this man
Who had ventured through hell my doom to revoke,
As only the truest of comrades can.
I begged him to tell me how best I might aid him,
And urgently prayed him
Never to leave me, whatever betide;
When I saw he was hurt —
Shot through the hands that were clasped in prayer!
Then, as the dark drops gathered there
And fell in the dirt,

The wounds of my friend
Seemed to me such as no man might bear.
Those bullet-holes in the patient hands
Seemed to transcend
All horrors that ever these war-drenched lands
Had known or would know till the mad world's end.
Then suddenly I was aware
That his feet had been wounded, too;
And, dimming the white of his side,
A dull stain grew.
"You are hurt, White Comrade!" I cried.
His words I already foreknew:
"These are old wounds," said he,
"But of late they have troubled me."

Robert Haven Schauffler

SMITH, OF THE THIRD OREGON, DIES [1]

AUTUMN in Oregon is wet as Spring,
And green, with little singings in the grass,
    And pheasants flying,
Gold, green and red,
Great, narrow, lovely things,
As if an orchid had snatched wings.
There are strange birds like blots against a sky
    Where a sun is dying.
Beyond the river where the hills are blurred
A cloud, like the one word
Of the too-silent sky, stirs, and there stand
    Black trees on either hand.

[1] Reprinted, by permission of the publishers, from *Drums in Our Street*, by Mary Carolyn Davies. Copyright. 1918, by the Macmillan Company.

Autumn in Oregon is wet and new
    As Spring,
And puts a fever like Spring's in the cheek
That once has touched her dew —
And it puts longing too
In eyes that once have seen
Her season-flouting green,
    And ears that listened to her strange birds
        speak.

Autumn in Oregon — I'll never see
Those hills again, a blur of blue and rain
Across the old Willamette. I'll not stir
A pheasant as I walk, and hear it whirr
Above my head, an indolent, trusting thing.
When all this silly dream is finished here,
The fellows will go home to where there fall
Rose-petals over every street, and all
The year is like a friendly festival.
But I shall never watch those hedges drip
Color, not see the tall spar of a ship
In our old harbor. — They say that I am dying,
Perhaps that's why it all comes back again:
Autumn in Oregon and pheasants flying —
         Mary Carolyn Davies

SONG

    SHE goes all so softly
        Like a shadow on the hill,
    A faint wind at twilight
        That stirs, and is still.

She weaves her thoughts whitely,
    Like doves in the air,
Though a gray mound in Flanders
    Clouds all that was fair.

Edward J. O'Brien

LONELY BURIAL

THERE were not many at that lonely place,
Where two scourged hills met in a little plain.
The wind cried loud in gusts, then low again.
Three pines strained darkly, runners in a race
Unseen by any. Toward the further woods
A dim harsh noise of voices rose and ceased.
— We were most silent in those solitudes —
Then, sudden as a flame, the black-robed priest
The clotted earth piled roughly up about
The hacked red oblong of the new-made thing,
Short words in swordlike Latin — and a rout
Of dreams most impotent, unwearying.
Then, like a blind door shut on a carouse,
The terrible bareness of the soul's last house.

Stephen Vincent Benét

I HAVE A RENDEZVOUS WITH DEATH

I HAVE a rendezvous with Death
At some disputed barricade,
When Spring comes back with rustling shade
And apple-blossoms fill the air —
I have a rendezvous with Death
When Spring brings back blue days and fair.

It may be he shall take my hand
And lead me into his dark land
And close my eyes and quench my breath —
It may be I shall pass him still.
I have a rendezvous with Death
On some scarred slope of battered hill
When Spring comes round again this year
And the first meadow-flowers appear.

God knows 't were better to be deep
Pillowed in silk and scented down,
Where Love throbs out in blissful sleep,
Pulse nigh to pulse, and breath to breath,
Where hushed awakenings are dear . . .
But I've a rendezvous with Death
At midnight in some flaming town,
When Spring trips north again this year,
And I to my pledged word am true,
I shall not fail that rendezvous.

Alan Seeger

ROUGE BOUQUET

In a wood they call the Rouge Bouquet
There is a new-made grave to-day,
Built by never a spade nor pick
Yet covered with earth ten metres thick.
There lie many fighting men,
    Dead in their youthful prime,
Never to laugh nor love again
    Nor taste the Summertime.
For Death came flying through the air
And stopped his flight at the dugout stair,

Touched his prey and left them there,
    Clay to clay.
He hid their bodies stealthily
In the soil of the land they fought to free
    And fled away.
Now over the grave abrupt and clear
    Three volleys ring;
And perhaps their brave young spirits hear
    The bugle sing:
"Go to sleep!
Go to sleep!
Slumber well where the shell screamed and fell.
Let your rifles rest on the muddy floor,
You will not need them any more.
Danger's past;
Now at last,
Go to sleep!"

There is on earth no worthier grave
To hold the bodies of the brave
Than this place of pain and pride
Where they nobly fought and nobly died.
Never fear but in the skies
Saints and angels stand
Smiling with their holy eyes
On this new-come band.
St. Michael's sword darts through the air
And touches the aureole on his hair
As he sees them stand saluting there,
    His stalwart sons;
And Patrick, Brigid, Columkill
Rejoice that in veins of warriors still
    The Gael's blood runs.

And up to Heaven's doorway floats,
From the wood called Rouge Bouquet,
A delicate cloud of buglenotes
That softly say:
"Farewell!
Farewell!
Comrades true, born anew, peace to you!
Your souls shall be where the heroes are
And your memory shine like the morning-star.
Brave and dear,
Shield us here.
Farewell!"

Joyce Kilmer

FRANCIS LEDWIDGE

(Killed in action July 31, 1917)

NEVERMORE singing
Will you go now,
Wearing wild moonlight
On your brow.
The moon's white mood
In your silver mind
Is all forgotten.
Words of wind
From off the hedgerow
After rain,
You do not hear them;
They are vain.
There is a linnet
Craves a song,
And you returning
Before long.

Now who will tell her,
Who can say
On what great errand
You are away?
You whose kindred
Were hills of Meath,
Who sang the lane-rose
From her sheath,
What voice will cry them
The grief at dawn
Or say to the blackbird
You are gone?

Grace Hazard Conkling

APRIL ON THE BATTLEFIELDS

APRIL now walks the fields again,
Trailing her tearful leaves
And holding all her frightened buds against her heart:
Wrapt in her clouds and mists,
She walks,
Groping her way among the graves of men.

The green of earth is differently green,
A dreadful knowledge trembles in the grass,
And little wide-eyed flowers die too soon:
There is a stillness here —
After a terror of all raving sounds —
And birds sit close for comfort upon the boughs
Of broken trees.

April, thou grief!
What of thy sun and glad, high wind,

Thy valiant hills and woods and eager brooks,
Thy thousand-petalled hopes?
The sky forbids thee sorrow, April!
And yet —
I see thee walking listlessly
Across those scars that once were joyous sod,
Those graves,
Those stepping-stones from life to life.

Death is an interruption between two heart-beats,
That I know —
Yet know not how I know —
But April mourns,
Trailing her tender green,
The passion of her green,
Across the passion of those fearful fields.

Yes, all the fields:
No barrier here,
No challenge in the night,
No stranger-land;
She passes with her perfect countersign,
Her green;
She wanders in her mournful garden,
Dropping her buds like tears,
Spreading her lovely grief upon the graves of man.

Leonora Speyer

EARTH'S EASTER
(1915)

EARTH has gone up from its Gethsemane,
    And now on Golgotha is crucified;
    The spear is twisted in the tortured side;
The thorny crown still works its cruelty.

Hark! while the victim suffers on the tree,
　　There sound through starry spaces, far and wide,
　　Such words as in the last despair are cried:
"My God! my God! Thou hast forsaken me!"

But when earth's members from the cross are drawn,
And all we love into the grave is gone,
　　This hope shall be a spark within the gloom:
That, in the glow of some stupendous dawn,
　　We may go forth to find, where lilies bloom,
　　Two angels bright before an empty tomb.

Robert Haven Schauffler

THE FIELDS

Though wisdom underfoot
　　Dies in the bloody fields,
Slowly the endless root
　　Gathers again and yields.

In fields where hate has hurled
　　Its force, where folly rots,
Wisdom shall be unfurled
　　Small as forget-me-nots.

Witter Bynner

IN SPITE OF WAR

In spite of war, in spite of death,
In spite of all man's sufferings,
Something within me laughs and sings
And I must praise with all my breath.
In spite of war, in spite of hate
Lilacs are blooming at my gate,

Tulips are tripping down the path
In spite of war, in spite of wrath.
"Courage!" the morning-glory saith;
"Rejoice!" the daisy murmureth,
And just to live is so divine
When pansies lift their eyes to mine.

The clouds are romping with the sea,
And flashing waves call back to me
That naught is real but what is fair,
That everywhere and everywhere
A glory liveth through despair.
Though guns may roar and cannon boom,
Roses are born and gardens bloom;
My spirit still may light its flame
At that same torch whence poppies came.
Where morning's altar whitely burns
Lilies may lift their silver urns
In spite of war, in spite of shame.

And in my ear a whispering breath,
"Wake from the nightmare! Look and see
That life is naught but ecstasy
In spite of war, in spite of death!"

Angela Morgan

WIDE HAVEN

TIRED of man's futile, petty cry,
Of lips that lie and flout,
I saw the slow sun dim and die
And the slim dusk slip out . . .
Life held no room for doubt.

What though Death claim the ones I prize
  In War's insane crusade,
Last night I saw Orion rise
  And the great day-star fade,
  And I am not dismayed.

Clement Wood

TO ANY ONE

WHETHER the time be slow or fast,
  Enemies, hand in hand,
Must come together at the last
  And understand.

No matter how the die is cast
  Nor who may seem to win,
You know that you must love at last —
  Why not begin?

Witter Bynner

PEACE

SUDDENLY bells and flags!
Suddenly — door to door —
Tidings! Can we believe,
We, who were used to war?

Yet we have dreamed her face,
Knowing her light must be,
Knowing that she must come.
Look — she comes, it is she!

Tattered her raiment floats,
Blood is upon her wings.

Ah, but her eyes are clear!
Ah, but her voice outrings!

Soon where the shrapnel fell
Petals shall wake and stir.
Look — she is here, she lives!
Beauty has died for her.

Agnes Lee

THE KINGS ARE PASSING DEATHWARD

THE Kings are passing deathward in the dark
  Of days that had been splendid where they went;
Their crowns are captive and their courts are stark
  Of purples that are ruinous, now, and rent.
For all that they have seen disastrous things:
  The shattered pomp, the split and shaken throne,
They cannot quite forget the way of Kings:
  Gravely they pass, majestic and alone.

With thunder on their brows, their faces set
  Toward the eternal night of restless shapes,
They walk in awful splendor, regal yet,
  Wearing their crimes like rich and kingly capes . . .
Curse them or taunt, they will not hear or see;
  The Kings are passing deathward: let them be.

David Morton

JERICO

JERICO, Jerico,
Round and round the walls I go
Where they watch with scornful eyes,
Where the captained bastions rise;

Heel and toe, heel and toe,
Blithely round the walls I go.

Jerico, Jerico,
Round and round the walls I go . . .
All the golden ones of earth
Regal in their lordly mirth . . .
Heel and toe, heel and toe,
Round and round the walls I go.

Jerico, Jerico,
Blithely round the walls I go,
With a broken sword in hand
Where the mighty bastions stand;
Heel and toe, heel and toe,
Hear my silly bugle blow.

Heel and toe, heel and toe,
Round the walls of Jerico . . .
Past the haughty golden gate
Where the emperor in state
Smiles to see the ragged show,
Round and round the towers go.

Jerico, Jerico,
Round and round and round I go . . .
All their sworded bodies must
Lie low in their tower's dust . . .
Heel and toe, heel and toe,
Blithely round the walls I go.

Heel and toe, heel and toe, —
I will blow a thunder note

From my brazen bugle's throat
Till the sand and thistle know
The leveled walls of Jerico,
Jerico, Jerico, Jerico, . . .

Willard Wattles

STUDENTS

JOHN BROWN and Jeanne at Fontainebleau —
'T was Toussaint, just a year ago;
Crimson and copper was the glow
Of all the woods at Fontainebleau.
They peered into that ancient well,
And watched the slow torch as it fell.
John gave the keeper two whole sous,
And Jeanne that smile with which she woos
John Brown to folly. So they lose
The Paris train. But never mind! —
All-Saints are rustling in the wind,
And there's an inn, a crackling fire —
(It's *deux-cinquante*, but Jeanne's desire);
There's dinner, candles, country wine,
Jeanne's lips — philosophy divine!

There was a bosquet at Saint Cloud
Wherein John's picture of her grew
To be a Salon masterpiece —
Till the rain fell that would not cease.
Through one long alley how they raced! —
'T was gold and brown, and all a waste
Of matted leaves, moss-interlaced.
Shades of mad queens and hunter-kings
And thorn-sharp feet of dryad-things

Were company to their wanderings;
Then rain and darkness on them drew.
The rich folks' motors honked and flew.
They hailed an old cab, heaven for two;
The bright Champs-Elysées at last —
Though the cab crawled it sped too fast.

Paris, upspringing white and gold:
Flamboyant arch and high-enscrolled
War-sculpture, big, Napoleonic —
Fierce chargers, angels histrionic;
The royal sweep of gardened spaces,
The pomp and whirl of columned Places;
The *Rive Gauche*, age-old, gay and gray;
The *impasse* and the loved café;
The tempting tidy little shops;
The convent walls, the glimpsed tree-tops;
Book-stalls, old men like dwarfs in plays;
Talk, work, and Latin Quarter ways.

May — Robinson's, the chestnut trees —
Were ever crowds as gay as these?
The quick pale waiters on a run,
The round, green tables, one by one,
Hidden away in amorous bowers —
Lilac, laburnum's golden showers.
Kiss, clink of glasses, laughter heard,
And nightingales quite undeterred.
And then that last extravagance —
O Jeanne, a single amber glance
Will pay him! — "Let's play millionaire
For just two hours — on princely fare,

At some hotel where lovers dine
À *deux* and pledge across the wine!"
They find a damask breakfast-room,
Where stiff silk roses range their bloom.
The *garcon* has a splendid way
Of bearing in *grand déjeuner.*
Then to be left alone, alone,
High up above Rue Castiglione;
Curtained away from all the rude
Rumors, in silken solitude;
And, John, her head upon your knees —
Time waits for moments such as these.

Florence Wilkinson

TAMPICO

OH, cut me reeds to blow upon,
    Or gather me a star,
But leave the sultry passion-flowers
    Growing where they are.

I fear their sombre yellow deeps,
    Their whirling fringe of black,
And he who gives a passion-flower
    Always asks it back.

Grace Hazard Conkling

WHICH

WE ask that Love shall rise to the divine,
And yet we crave him very human, too;
Our hearts would drain the crimson of his wine,
Our souls despise him if he prove untrue!

Poor Love! I hardly see what you can do!
We know all human things are weak and frail,
And yet we claim that very part of you,
Then, inconsistent, blame you if you fail.
When you would soar, 't is we who clip your wings,
Although we weep because you faint and fall.
Alas! it seems we want so many things,
That no dear love could ever grant them all!
Which shall we choose, the human or divine,
The crystal stream, or yet the crimson wine?

Corinne Roosevelt Robinson

APOLOGY [1]

BE not angry with me that I bear
    Your colours everywhere,
      All through each crowded street,
        And meet
    The wonder-light in every eye,
      As I go by.

Each plodding wayfarer looks up to gaze,
    Blinded by rainbow haze,
    The stuff of happiness,
      No less,
    Which wraps me in its glad-hued folds
      Of peacock golds.

Before my feet the dusty, rough-paved way
    Flushes beneath its gray.

My steps fall ringed with light,
     So bright,
It seems a myriad suns are strown
     About the town.

Around me is the sound of steepled bells,
     And rich perfuméd smells
Hang like a wind-forgotten cloud,
     And shroud
Me from close contact with the world.
     I dwell impearled.

You blazen me with jewelled insignia.
     A flaming nebula
Rims in my life. And yet
     You set
The word upon me, unconfessed
     To go unguessed.

Amy Lowell

THE GREAT HUNT

I CANNOT tell you now;
     When the wind's drive and whirl
     Blow me along no longer,
     And the wind's a whisper at last —
Maybe I'll tell you then —

                    some other time.

     When the rose's flash to the sunset
     Reels to the wrack and the twist,
     And the rose is a red bygone,
     When the face I love is going

And the gate to the end shall clang,
  And it's no use to beckon or say, "So long" —
Maybe I'll tell you then —

                      some other time.

I never knew any more beautiful than you:
  I have hunted you under my thoughts,
  I have broken down under the wind
  And into the roses looking for you.
    I shall never find any

                      greater than you.
                      Carl Sandburg

DIALOGUE

BE patient, Life, when Love is at the gate,
And when he enters let him be at home.
Think of the roads that he has had to roam.
Think of the years that he has had to wait.

But if I let Love in I shall be late.
Another has come first — there is no room.
And I am thoughtful of the endless loom —
Let Love be patient, the importunate.

O Life, be idle and let Love come in,
And give thy dreamy hair that Love may spin.

But Love himself is idle with his song.
Let Love come last, and then may Love last long.

Be patient, Life, for Love is not the last.
Be patient now with Death, for Love has passed.
                      Walter Conrad Arensberg

SONG

THE Spring will come when the year turns,
   As if no Winter had been,
But what shall I do with a locked heart
   That lets no new year in?

The birds will go when the Fall goes,
   The leaves will fade in the field,
But what shall I do with an old love
   Will neither die nor yield?

Oh! youth will turn as the world turns,
   And dim grow laughter and pain,
But how shall I hide from an old dream
   I never may dream again?

Margaret Widdemer

THE BITTER HERB

O BITTER herb, Forgetfulness,
I search for you in vain;
You are the only growing thing
Can take away my pain.

When I was young, this bitter herb
Grew wild on every hill;
I should have plucked a store of it,
And kept it by me still.

I hunt through all the meadows
Where once I wandered free,
But the rare herb, Forgetfulness,
It hides away from me.

O bitter herb, Forgetfulness,
Where is your drowsy breath?
Oh, can it be your seed has blown
Far as the Vales of Death?
Jeanne Robert Foster

BEHIND THE HOUSE IS THE MILLET PLOT

BEHIND the house is the millet plot,
And past the millet, the stile;
And then a hill where melilot
Grows with wild camomile.

There was a youth who bade me goodby
Where the hill rises to meet the sky.
I think my heart broke; but I have forgot
All but the smell of the white melilot.
Muna Lee

MEN OF HARLAN

HERE in the level country, where the creeks run
straight and wide,
Six men upon their pacing nags may travel side by
side.
But the mountain men of Harlan, you may tell them
all the while,
When they pass through our village, for they ride in
single file.
And the children, when they see them, stop their play
and stand and cry,
"Here come the men of Harlan, men of Harlan, riding
by!"

O the mountain men of Harlan, when they come down
    to the plain,
With dangling stirrup, jangling spur, and loosely
    hanging rein,
They do not ride, like our folks here, in twos and
    threes abreast,
With merry laughter, talk and song, and lightly spoken
    jest;
But silently and solemnly, in long and straggling line,
As you may see them in the hills, beyond Big Black
    and Pine.

For, in that far strange country, where the men of
    Harlan dwell,
There are no roads at all, like ours, as we've heard
    travelers tell.
But only narrow trails that wind along each shallow
    creek,
Where the silence hangs so heavy, you can hear the
    leathers squeak.
And there no two can ride abreast, but each alone
    must go,
Picking his way as best he may, with careful steps and
    slow,

Down many a shelving ledge of shale, skirting the
    trembling sands,
Through many a pool and many a pass, where the
    mountain laurel stands
So thick and close to left and right, with holly bushes,
    too,
The clinging branches meet midway to bar the passage
    through, —

O'er many a steep and stony ridge, o'er many a high
    divide,
And so it is the Harlan men thus one by one do ride.

Yet it is strange to see them pass in line through our
    wide street,
When they come down to sell their sang, and buy their
    stores of meat,
These silent men, in sombre black, all clad from foot
    to head,
Though they have left their lonely hills and the nar-
    row creek's rough bed.
And 't is no wonder children stop their play and stand
    and cry:
"Here come the men of Harlan, men of Harlan, riding
    by."

William Aspinwall Bradley

HAVE YOU AN EYE

HAVE you an eye for the trails, the trails,
    The old mark and the new?
What scurried here, what loitered there,
    In the dust and in the dew?

Have you an eye for the beaten track,
    The old hoof and the young?
Come name me the drivers of yesterday,
    Sing me the songs they sung.

O, was it a schooner last went by,
    And where will it ford the stream?
Where will it halt in the early dusk,
    And where will the camp-fire gleam?

They used to take the shortest cut
    The cattle trails had made;
Get down the hill by the easy slope
    To the water and the shade.

But it's barbed wire fence, and section line,
    And kill-horse travel now;
Scoot you down the canyon bank, —
    The old road 's under plough.

Have you an eye for the laden wheel,
    The worn tire or the new?
Or the sign of the prairie pony's hoof
    Was never trimmed for shoe?

Edwin Ford Piper

AFTER APPLE-PICKING

My long two-pointed ladder 's sticking through a tree
Toward heaven still,
And there's a barrel that I did n't fill
Beside it, and there may be two or three
Apples I did n't pick upon some bough.
But I am done with apple-picking now.
Essence of winter sleep is on the night,
The scent of apples: I am drowsing off.
I cannot rub the strangeness from my sight
I got from looking through a pane of glass
I skimmed this morning from the drinking trough
And held against the world of hoary grass.
It melted, and I let it fall and break.
But I was well
Upon my way to sleep before it fell,
And I could tell

What form my dreaming was about to take.
Magnified apples appear and disappear,
Stem end and blossom end,
And every fleck of russet showing clear.
My instep arch not only keeps the ache,
It keeps the pressure of a ladder-round.
I feel the ladder sway as the boughs bend.
And I keep hearing from the cellar bin
The rumbling sound
Of load on load of apples coming in.
For I have had too much
Of apple-picking: I am overtired
Of the great harvest I myself desired.
There were ten thousand thousand fruit to touch,
Cherish in hand, lift down, and not let fall.
For all
That struck the earth,
No matter if not bruised or spiked with stubble,
Went surely to the cider-apple heap
As of no worth.
One can see what will trouble
This sleep of mine, whatever sleep it is.
Were he not gone,
The woodchuck could say whether it's like his
Long sleep, as I describe its coming on,
Or just some human sleep.

Robert Frost

AUTUMN

(*For my Mother*)

How memory cuts away the years,
And how clean the picture comes
Of autumn days, brisk and busy;

Charged with keen sunshine.
And you, stirred with activity;
The spirit of these energetic days.

There was our back-yard,
So plain and stripped of green,
With even the weeds carefully pulled away
From the crooked, red bricks that made the walk.
And the earth on either side so black.

Autumn and dead leaves burning in the sharp air;
And winter comforts coming in like a pageant.
I shall not forget them:
Great jars laden with the raw green of pickles,
Standing in a solemn row across the back of the porch,
Exhaling the pungent dill;
And in the very center of the yard,
You, tending the great catsup kettle of gleaming
      copper
Where fat, red tomatoes bobbed up and down
Like jolly monks in a drunken dance.
And there were bland banks of cabbages that came by
      the wagon-load,
Soon to be cut into delicate ribbons
Only to be crushed by the heavy, wooden stompers.
Such feathery whiteness — to come to kraut!
And after, there were grapes that hid their brightness
      under a grey dust,
Then gushed thrilling, purple blood over the fire;
And enamelled crab-apples that tricked with their
      fragrance
But were bitter to taste.
And there were spicy plums and ill-shaped quinces,

And long string beans floating in pans of clear water
Like slim, green fishes.
And there was fish itself,
Salted, silver herring from the city . . .

And you moved among these mysteries,
Absorbed and smiling and sure;
Stirring, tasting, measuring,
With the precision of a ritual.
I like to think of you in your years of power —
You, now so shaken and so powerless —
High priestess of your home.

Jean Starr Untermeyer

AUTUMN MOVEMENT

I CRIED over beautiful things knowing no beautiful
thing lasts.

The field of cornflower yellow is a scarf at the neck of
the copper sunburned woman, the mother of
the year, the taker of seeds.

The northwest wind comes and the yellow is torn full
of holes, new beautiful things come in the first
spit of snow on the northwest wind, and the old
things go, not one lasts.

Carl Sandburg

GOD'S WORLD

O WORLD, I cannot hold thee close enough!
Thy winds, thy wide grey skies!
Thy mists that roll and rise!

Thy woods this autumn day, that ache and sag
And all but cry with colour! That gaunt crag
To crush! To lift the lean of that black bluff!
World, World, I cannot get thee close enough!

Long have I known a glory in it all,
    But never knew I this;
    Here such a passion is
As stretcheth me apart, — Lord, I do fear
Thou'st made the world too beautiful this year;
My soul is all but out of me, — let fall
No burning leaf; prithee, let no bird call.
                    Edna St. Vincent Millay

OVERTONES

I HEARD a bird at break of day
    Sing from the autumn trees
A song so mystical and calm,
    So full of certainties,
No man, I think, could listen long
    Except upon his knees.
Yet this was but a simple bird,
    Alone, among dead trees.
                  William Alexander Percy

WHEN THE YEAR GROWS OLD

I CANNOT but remember
    When the year grows old —
October — November —
    How she disliked the cold!

She used to watch the swallows
    Go down across the sky,
And turn from the window
    With a little sharp sigh.

And often when the brown leaves
    Were brittle on the ground,
And the wind in the chimney
    Made a melancholy sound,

She had a look about her
    That I wish I could forget —
The look of a scared thing
    Sitting in a net!

Oh, beautiful at nightfall
    The soft spitting snow!
And beautiful the bare boughs
    Rubbing to and fro!

But the roaring of the fire,
    And the warmth of fur,
And the boiling of the kettle
    Were beautiful to her!

I cannot but remember
    When the year grows old —
October — November —
    How she disliked the cold!
               Edna St. Vincent Millay

IN THE MONASTERY

COLD is the wind to-night, and rough the sea,
Too rough for even the daring Dane to find
A landing-place upon the frozen lea.

> Cold is the wind.

The blast sweeps round the chapel from behind,
Making the altar-light flare fitfully,
While I must kneel and pray with troubled mind.

Patrick and Brigid, I have prayed to ye!
The night is over, and my task resigned
To Colum. Though God's own dwelling shelter me,

> Cold is the wind.

Norreys Jephson O'Conor

THE NARROW DOORS

THE Wide Door into Sorrow
Stands open night and day.
With head held high and dancing feet
I pass it on my way.

I never tread within it,
I never turn to see
The Wide Door into Sorrow.
It cannot frighten me.

The Narrow Doors to Sorrow
Are secret, still, and low:
Swift tongues of dusk that spoil the sun
Before I even know.

My dancing feet are frozen.
I stare. I can but see.
The Narrow Doors to Sorrow
They stop the heart in me.

— Oh, stranger than my midnights
Of loneliness and strife
The Doors that let the dark leap in
Across my sunny life!

Fannie Stearns Davis

I PASS A LIGHTED WINDOW

I PASS a lighted window
    And a closed door —
And I am not troubled
    Any more.

Though the road is murky,
    I am not afraid,
For a shadow passes
    On the lighted shade.

Once I knew the sesame
    To the closed door;
Now I shall not enter
    Any more;

Nor will people passing
    By the lit place,
See our shadows marry
    In a gray embrace.

Strange a passing shadow
　　Has a long spell!
What can matter, knowing
　　She does well?

How can life annoy me
　　Any more?
Life: a lighted window
　　And a closed door.

Clement Wood

DOORS [1]

LIKE a young child who to his mother's door
　　Runs eager for the welcoming embrace,
　　And finds the door shut, and with troubled face
Calls and through sobbing calls, and o'er and o'er
Calling, storms at the panel — so before
　　A door that will not open, sick and numb,
　　I listen for a word that will not come,
And know, at last, I may not enter more.

Silence! And through the silence and the dark
　　By that closed door, the distant sob of tears
　　Beats on my spirit, as on fairy shores
The spectral sea; and through the sobbing — hark!
　　Down the fair-chambered corridor of years,
　　The quiet shutting, one by one, of doors.

Hermann Hagedorn

[1] Reprinted, by permission of the publishers, from *Poems and Ballads* by Hermann Hagedorn. Copyright 1913, by The Macmillan Company.

WHERE LOVE ONCE WAS

WHERE love once was, let there be no hate:
Though they that went as one by night and day
Go now alone,
Where love once was, let there be no hate.

The seeds we planted together
Came to rich harvest,
And our hearts are as bins brimming with the golden
      plenty:
Into our loneliness we carry granaries of old love . . .

And though the time has come when we cannot sow
      our acres together,
And our souls need diverse fields,
And a tilling apart,
Let us go separate ways with a blessing each for each,
And gentle parting,
And let there be no hate,
Where love once was.

James Oppenheim

IRISH LOVE SONG

WELL, if the thing is over, better it is for me,
The lad was ever a rover, loving and laughing free,
Far too clever a lover not to be having still
A lass in the town and a lass by the road and a lass
      by the farther hill —
Love on the field and love on the path and love in the
      woody glen —
(Lad, will I never see you, never your face again?)

Ay, if the thing is ending, now I'll be getting rest,
Saying my prayers and bending down to be stilled and
    blest,
Never the days are sending hope till my heart is
    sore
For a laugh on the path and a voice by the gate and a
    step on the shieling floor —
Grief on my ways and grief on my work and grief till
    the evening's dim —
(Lord, will I never hear it, never a sound of him?)

Sure if it's done forever, better for me that's wise,
Never the hurt, and never tears in my aching eyes,
No more the trouble ever to hide from my asking
    folk
Beat of my heart at click o' the latch, and throb if
    his name is spoke;
Never the need to hide the sighs and the flushing
    thoughts and the fret,
And after awhile my heart will hush and my hungering
    hands forget . . .
Peace on my ways, and peace in my step, and maybe
    my heart grown light —
(*Mary, helper of heartbreak, send him to me to-night!*)
                   Margaret Widdemer

NIRVANA

Sleep on — I lie at heaven's high oriels,
    Over the stars that murmur as they go
    Lighting your lattice-window far below;
And every star some of the glory spells
    Whereof I know.

I have forgotten you, long long ago;
    Like the sweet, silver singing of thin bells
Vanished, or music fading faint and low.
    Sleep on — I lie at heaven's high oriels,
Who loved you so.

                  John Hall Wheelock

A NUN

ONE glance and I had lost her in the riot
    Of tangled cries.
She trod the clamor with a cloistral quiet
    Deep in her eyes
As though she heard the muted music only
    That silence makes
Among dim mountain summits and on lonely
    Deserted lakes.

There is some broken song her heart remembers
    From long ago,
Some love lies buried deep, some passion's embers
    Smothered in snow,
Far voices of a joy that sought and missed her
    Fail now, and cease . . .
And this has given the deep eyes of God's sister
    Their dreadful peace.

                  Odell Shepard

SILENCE [1]

I HAVE known the silence of the stars and of the sea,
And the silence of the city when it pauses,
And the silence of a man and a maid,

[1] Reprinted, by permission of the publishers, from *Songs and Satires,* by Edgar Lee Masters. Copyright, 1915, by The Macmillan Company.

And the silence of the sick
When their eyes roam about the room.
And I ask: For the depths,
Of what use is language?
A beast of the field moans a few times
When death takes its young.
And we are voiceless in the presence of realities —
We cannot speak.

A curious boy asks an old soldier
Sitting in front of the grocery store,
"How did you lose your leg?"
And the old soldier is struck with silence,
Or his mind flies away
Because he cannot concentrate it on Gettysburg.
It comes back jocosely
And he says, "A bear bit it off."
And the boy wonders, while the old soldier
Dumbly, feebly lives over
The flashes of guns, the thunder of cannon,
The shrieks of the slain,
And himself lying on the ground,
And the hospital surgeons, the knives,
And the long days in bed.
But if he could describe it all
He would be an artist.
But if he were an artist there would be deeper
        wounds
Which he could not describe.

There is the silence of a great hatred,
And the silence of a great love,
And the silence of an embittered friendship.

There is the silence of a spiritual crisis,
Through which your soul, exquisitely tortured,
Comes with visions not to be uttered
Into a realm of higher life.
There is the silence of defeat.
There is the silence of those unjustly punished;
And the silence of the dying whose hand
Suddenly grips yours.
There is the silence between father and son,
When the father cannot explain his life,
Even though he be misunderstood for it.

There is the silence that comes between husband and
     wife.
There is the silence of those who have failed;
And the vast silence that covers
Broken nations and vanquished leaders.
There is the silence of Lincoln,
Thinking of the poverty of his youth.
And the silence of Napoleon
After Waterloo.
And the silence of Jeanne d'Arc
Saying amid the flames, "Blessed Jesus"—
Revealing in two words all sorrows, all hope.
And there is the silence of age,
Too full of wisdom for the tongue to utter it
In words intelligible to those who have not lived
The great range of life.

And there is the silence of the dead.
If we who are in life cannot speak
Of profound experiences,
Why do you marvel that the dead

Do not tell you of death?
Their silence shall be interpreted
As we approach them.

Edgar Lee Masters

THE DARK CAVALIER

I AM the Dark Cavalier; I am the Last Lover:
  My arms shall welcome you when other arms are
    tired;
I stand to wait for you, patient in the darkness,
  Offering forgetfulness of all that you desired.

I ask no merriment, no pretense of gladness,
  I can love heavy lids and lips without their rose;
Though you are sorrowful you will not weary me;
  I will not go from you when all the tired world goes.

I am the Dark Cavalier; I am the Last Lover;
  I promise faithfulness no other lips may keep;
Safe in my bridal place, comforted by darkness,
  You shall lie happily, smiling in your sleep.

Margaret Widdemer

INDIAN SUMMER

(After completing a book for one now dead)

(O Earth-and-Autumn of the Setting Sun,
She is not by, to know my task is done.)
In the brown grasses slanting with the wind,
Lone as a lad whose dog's no longer near,
Lone as a mother whose only child has sinned,
Lone on the loved hill . . . and below me here

The thistle-down in tremulous atmosphere
Along red clusters of the sumach streams;
The shrivelled stalks of golden-rod are sere,
And crisp and white their flashing old racemes.
(. . . forever . . . forever . . . . forever . . .)
This is the lonely season of the year,
This is the season of our lonely dreams.

(O Earth-and-Autumn of the Setting Sun,
She is not by, to know my task is done!)
The corn-shocks westward on the stubble plain
Show like an Indian village of dead days;
The long smoke trails behind the crawling train,
And floats atop the distant woods ablaze
With orange, crimson, purple. The low haze
Dims the scarped bluffs above the inland sea,
Whose wide and slaty waters in cold glaze
Await yon full-moon of the night-to-be,
(. . . far . . . and far . . . and far . . .)
These are the solemn horizons of man's ways,
These are the horizons of solemn thought to me.

(O Earth-and-Autumn of the Setting Sun,
She is not by, to know my task is done!)
And this the hill she visited, as friend;
And this the hill she lingered on, as bride —
Down in the yellow valley is the end:
They laid her . . . in no evening autumn tide . . .
Under fresh flowers of that May morn, beside
The queens and cave-women of ancient earth . . .

This is the hill . . . and over my city's towers,
Across the world from sunset, yonder in air,

Shines, through its scaffoldings, a civic dome
Of pilèd masonry, which shall be ours
To give, completed, to our children there . . .
And yonder far roof of my abandoned home
Shall house new laughter . . . Yet I tried . . . I tried
And, ever wistful of the doom to come,
I built her many a fire for love . . . for mirth . . .
(When snows were falling on our oaks outside,
Dear, many a winter fire upon the hearth) . . .
(. . . farewell . . . farewell . . . farewell . . .)
We dare not think too long on those who died,
While still so many yet must come to birth.

William Ellery Leonard

DEATH —DIVINATION

Death is like moonlight in a lofty wood,
    That pours pale magic through the shadowy leaves;
    'T is like the web that some old perfume weaves
In a dim, lonely room where memories brood;
Like snow-chilled wine it steals into the blood,
    Spurring the pulse its coolness half reprieves;
    Tenderly quickening impulses it gives,
As April winds unsheathe an opening bud.

Death is like all sweet, sense-enfolding things,
    That lift us in a dream-delicious trance
    Beyond the flickering good and ill of chance;
But most is Death like Music's buoyant wings,
    That bear the soul, a willing Ganymede,
    Where joys on joys forevermore succeed.

Charles Wharton Stork

THE MOULD

No doubt this active will,
So bravely steeped in sun,
This will has vanquished Death
And foiled oblivion.

But this indifferent clay,
This fine experienced hand,
So quiet, and these thoughts
That all unfinished stand,

Feel death as though it were
A shadowy caress;
And win and wear a frail
Archaic wistfulness.

Gladys Cromwell

IN PATRIS MEI MEMORIAM

By the fond name that was his own and mine,
  The last upon his lips that strove with doom,
  He called me and I saw the light assume
A sudden glory and around him shine;
And nearer now I saw the laureled line
  Of the august of Song before me loom,
  And knew the voices, erstwhile through the
    gloom,
That whispered and forbade me to repine.
And with farewell, a shaft of splendor sank
  Out of the stars and faded as a flame,

And down the night, on clouds of glory, came
The battle seraphs halting rank on rank;
And lifted heavenward to heroic peace,
    He passed and left me hope beyond surcease.
                                    John Myers O'Hara

AD MATREM AMANTISSIMAM ET CARISSIMAM FILII IN ÆTERNUM FIDELITAS

WITH all the fairest angels nearest God,
    The ineffable true of heart around the throne,
    There shall I find you waiting when the flown
Dream leaves my heart insentient as the clod;
And when the grief-retracing ways I trod
    Become a shining path to thee alone,
    My weary feet, that seemed to drag as stone,
Shall once again, with wings of fleetness shod,
Fare on, beloved, to find you! Just beyond
    The seraph throng await me, standing near
    The gentler angels, eager and apart;
Be there, near God's own fairest, with the fond
Sweet smile that was your own, and let me hear
    Your voice again and clasp you to my heart.
                                    John Myers O'Hara

AFTERWARDS

THERE was a day when death to me meant tears,
    And tearful takings-leave that had to be,
    And awed embarkings on an unshored sea,
And sudden disarrangement of the years.
But now I know that nothing interferes

With the fixed forces when a tired man dies;
That death is only answerings and replies,
The chiming of a bell which no one hears,
The casual slanting of a half-spent sun,
The soft recessional of noise and coil,
The coveted something time nor age can spoil;
I know it is a fabric finely spun
Between the stars and dark; to seize and keep,
Such glad romances as we read in sleep.

Mahlon Leonard Fisher

PIERRETTE IN MEMORY

PIERRETTE has gone, but it was not
    Exactly that she died,
So much as vanished and forgot
    To tell where she would hide.

To keep a sudden rendezvous,
    It came into her mind
That she was late. What could she **do**
    But leave distress behind?

Afraid of being in disgrace,
    And hurrying to dress,
She heard there was another place
    In need of loveliness.

She went so softly and so soon,
    She hardly made a stir;
But going took the stars and moon
    And sun away with her.

William Griffith

THE THREE SISTERS

Gone are the three, those sisters rare
  With wonder-lips and eyes ashine.
One was wise and one was fair,
  And one was mine.

Ye mourners, weave for the sleeping hair
  Of only two, your ivy vine.
For one was wise and one was fair,
  But one was mine.

Arthur Davison Ficke

SONG

I make my shroud, but no one knows —
So shimmering fine it is and fair,
With stitches set in even rows,
I make my shroud, but no one knows.

In door-way where the lilac blows,
Humming a little wandering air,
I make my shroud and no one knows,
So shimmering fine it is and fair.

Adelaide Crapsey

THE UNKNOWN BELOVÈD

I dreamed I passed a doorway
  Where, for a sign of death,
White ribbons one was binding
  About a flowery wreath.

What drew me so I know not,
    But drawing near I said,
"Kind sir, and can you tell me
    Who is it here lies dead?"

Said he, "Your most belovèd
    Died here this very day,
That had known twenty Aprils
    Had she but lived till May."

Astonished I made answer,
    "Good sir, how say you so!
Here have I no belovèd,
    This house I do not know."

Quoth he, "Who from the world's end
    Was destined unto thee
Here lies, thy true belovèd
    Whom thou shalt never see."

I dreamed I passed a doorway
    Where, for a sign of death,
White ribbons one was binding
    About a flowery wreath.
                        John Hall Wheelock

CINQUAINS

FATE DEFIED

As it
Were tissue of silver
I'll wear, O fate, thy grey,

And go mistily radiant, clad
Like the moon.

NIGHT WINDS

The old
Old winds that blew
When chaos was, what do
They tell the clattered trees that I
Should weep?

THE WARNING

Just now,
Out of the strange
Still dusk . . . as strange, as still . . .
A white moth flew . . . Why am I grown
So cold?

Adelaide Crapsey

THE LONELY DEATH

In the cold I will rise, I will bathe
In waters of ice; myself
Will shiver, and shrive myself,
Alone in the dawn, and anoint
Forehead and feet and hands;
I will shutter the windows from light,
I will place in their sockets the four
Tall candles and set them aflame
In the grey of the dawn; and myself
Will lay myself straight in my bed,
And draw the sheet under my chin.

Adelaide Crapsey

EXILE FROM GOD

I DO not fear to lay my body down
  In death, to share
The life of the dark earth and lose my own,
  If God is there.

I have so loved all sense of Him, sweet might
  Of color and sound, —
His tangible loveliness and living light
  That robes me 'round.

If to His heart in the hushed grave and dim
  We sink more near,
It shall be well — living we rest in Him.
  Only I fear

Lest from my God in lonely death I lapse,
  And the dumb clod
Lose him; for God is life, and death perhaps
  Exile from God.

John Hall Wheelock

LOAM

In the loam we sleep,
In the cool moist loam,
To the lull of years that pass
And the break of stars.

From the loam, then,
The soft warm loam,
  We rise:
To shape of rose leaf,
Of face and shoulder.

We stand, then,
To a whiff of life,
Lifted to the silver of the sun
Over and out of the loam
A day.

Carl Sandburg

HILLS OF HOME

NAME me no names for my disease,
With uninforming breath;
I tell you I am none of these,
But homesick unto death —

Homesick for hills that I had known,
For brooks that I had crossed,
Before I met this flesh and bone
And followed and was lost. . . .

And though they break my heart at last,
Yet name no name of ills.
Say only, "Here is where he passed,
Seeking again those hills."

Witter Bynner

THE LAST PIPER

DARK winds of the mountain,
White winds of the sea,
Are skirling the pibroch
Of Seumas an Righ.

The crying of gannets,
The shrieking of terns,
Are keening his dying
High over the burns.

Grey silence of waters
And wasting of lands
And the wailing of music
Down to the sands,

The wailing of music,
And trailing of wind,
The waters before him,
The mountains behind, —

Alone at the gathering,
Silent he stands,
And the wail of his piping
Cries over the lands,

To the moan of the waters,
The drone of the foam,
Where his soul, a white gannet,
Wings silently home.

Edward J. O'Brien

THE PROVINCES

O God that I
  May arise with the Gael
To the song in the sky
  Over Inisfail!

Ulster, your dark
Mold for me;
Munster, a lark
Hold for me!

Connaght, a *caoine*
Croon for me;
Lienster, a mean
Stone for me!

O God that I
May arise with the Gael
To the song in the sky
Over Inisfail!

Francis Carlin

OMNIUM EXEUNT IN MYSTERIUM

THE stranger in my gates — lo! that am I,
And what my land of birth I do not know,
Nor yet the hidden land to which I go.
One may be lord of many ere he die,
And tell of many sorrows in one sigh,
But know himself he shall not, nor his woe,
Nor to what sea the tears of wisdom flow;
Nor why one star is taken from the sky.
An urging is upon him evermore,
And though he bide, his soul is wanderer,
Scanning the shadows with a sense of haste —
Where fade the tracks of all who went before:
A dim and solitary traveller
On ways that end in evening and the waste.

George Sterling

MOTH-TERROR

I HAVE killed the moth flying around my night-light;
    wingless and dead it lies upon the floor.
(O who will kill the great Time-Moth that eats holes
    in my soul and that burrows in and through
    my secretest veils!)
My will against its will, and no more will it fly at my
    night-light or be hidden behind the curtains
    that swing in the winds.
(But O who will shatter the Change-Moth that leaves
    me in rags — tattered old tapestries that swing
    in the winds that blow out of Chaos!)
Night-Moth, Change-Moth, Time-Moth, eaters of
    dreams and of me!

Benjamin De Casseres

OLD AGE

I HAVE heard the wild geese,
I have seen the leaves fall,
There was frost last night
On the garden wall.
It is gone to-day
And I hear the wind call.
The wind? . . .That is all.

If the swallow will light
When the evening is near;
If the crane will not scream
Like a soul in fear;

I will think no more
Of the dying year,
And the wind, its seer.

Cale Young Rice

ATROPOS

Atropos, dread
   One of the Three,
Holding the thread
   Woven for me;

Grimly thy shears,
   Steely and bright,
Menace the years
   Left for delight.

Grant it may chance,
   Just as they close,
June may entrance
   Earth with the rose;

Reigning as though,
   Bliss to the breath,
Endless and no
   Whisper of death.

John Myers O'Hare

INDEX OF AUTHORS

INDEX OF FIRST LINES